THE**FIRST**100**CHORDS** **FOR**UKULELE

How to Learn and Play Ukulele Chords for Beginners

DARYL**KELLIE**

FUNDAMENTAL**CHANGES**

The First 100 Chords for Ukulele

How to Learn and Play Ukulele Chords for Beginners

ISBN: 978-1-78933-225-4

Published by **www.fundamental-changes.com**

www.fundamental-changes.com

Over 12,000 fans on Facebook: **FundamentalChangesInGuitar**

Instagram: **FundamentalChanges**

For over 350 Free Guitar Lessons with Videos Check Out

www.fundamental-changes.com

Cover Image Copyright: Shutterstock – megaflop / Tanakax3

Contents

Introduction   4

Get the Audio & Video   5

How to Read Chord Diagrams   6

Chapter One: C Major and F Major   8

Chapter Two: Adding Rhythm   13

Chapter Three: The "Three-Chord Trick"   20

Chapter Four: C, G, Am and F   26

Chapter Five: Introducing D Major   32

Chapter Six: Introducing E7   37

Chapter Seven: Introducing A Major   42

Chapter Eight: Dominant 7th Chords and The Blues   48

Chapter Nine: More Minor Chords   54

Chapter Ten: Moveable Chords   60

Chapter Eleven: Moveable 7ths and Minor 7ths   69

Chapter Twelve: Tricks, Crazy Chords and more!   78

Chapter Thirteen: Finishing Touches   91

Chord Dictionary and Closing Words   97

Introduction

The story of the ukulele began in 1879, when Portuguese immigrants arrived in Hawaii, bringing with them a tiny guitar-like instrument often referred to as a *machête*. The locals soon began producing their own version of this instrument using native koa wood.

The word ukulele means "jumping flea" in Hawaiian and there are many theories as to where this unusual moniker came from. The most likely is that the instrument was a particular favourite of an official in the court of King Kalakaua – a former British army officer named Edward Purvis. His small stature earned him the nickname "jumping flea" and so the ukulele was born.

In 1915, Johnah Kumalae, a Hawaiian ukulele maker and musician, showcased the instrument at the Pan Pacific International Exhibition. The instrument went down a storm and soon became popular across the United States, becoming closely associated with Vaudeville entertainers in the USA and light entertainers like George Formby in the UK. After the advent of Rock 'n' Roll music, the ukulele fell out of favour with the masses for a few decades.

In the early 21st Century, the ukulele began to snowball in popularity – in part, perhaps due to the enormous popularity of Israel Kamakawiwoʻoleʻs rendition of *Somewhere Over the Rainbow* and YouTube sensations such as Jake Shimabukuro. Soon, everyone from Taylor Swift to grunge rock icon Eddie Vedder could be seen playing uke. For many its portability, affordability, and relative ease of playing make it an excellent instrument to start out on.

This book is designed to help you master the most important chords and strumming patterns used on ukulele – the building blocks of thousands of well-known songs. Once you get started, you will soon see that the same chord sequences are used over and over again, and that with just a few simple chords you can quickly be making music!

However, you will also see that this is more than a simple list of chords and strumming patterns – it's a whole ukulele learning method, structured so that as you progress through the book, your skills, technique and musicality will improve with each example.

Laki maikaʻi (good luck!)

Daryl Kellie

October 2020

Get the Audio

The audio files for this book are available to download for free from **www.fundamental-changes.com.** The link is in the top right-hand corner. Simply select this book title from the drop-down menu and follow the instructions to get the audio.

We recommend that you download the files directly to your computer, not to your tablet, and extract them there before adding them to your media library. You can then put them on your tablet, iPod or burn them to CD. On the download page there is a help PDF and we also provide technical support via the contact form.

For over 350 free guitar lessons with videos check out:

www.fundamental-changes.com

Over 12,000 fans on Facebook: **FundamentalChangesInGuitar**

Instagram: **FundamentalChanges**

Get the Video

Each of the performance tunes in this book has been captured on video, so you can see exactly how each one should be played. You can access them on the Fundamental Changes website here:

https://geni.us/ukulelevideos

Or, scan the QR code below to view them on your smartphone/tablet

How to Read Chord Diagrams

The following images show how the written notation of music relates to where you place your fingers on the ukulele to play a chord. In its most basic form, every ukulele chord can be written down as a simple diagram. The vertical lines below are the *strings* of the instrument, and the horizontal lines are the *frets* (metal bars). The black dots on the strings show where you should put your fingers to create notes and form chords.

Each black dot contains a number that indicates which *finger* you should use to play the string. If you're right handed, hold up your left hand with your palm towards you. Your thumb goes on the back of the ukulele neck and your fingers are numbered 1, 2, 3 and 4. Finger 1 is your index (pointing) finger and finger 4 is your pinkie. You can see this in the diagram below.

When you place your fingers down just behind each fret, always use the very tip to make contact with the strings. Avoid using the soft, flat pad of the finger as it won't make a good contact with the strings and will cause them to buzz or rattle.

The G Major chord below is labelled with all the information you'll see on a chord diagram. An open circle at the end of the string means you should strum that string even though it doesn't have a finger placed on it. If a string has an X written on it, then you should avoid sounding it when you strum.

The final diagram shows a bar/measure of music notation with the G Major chord written out as music and tablature. Most of the time you won't need to worry about the dots or numbers on the notation, you can simply read the chord name that's written on top and strum the chord as shown.

However, the tablature is handy because it quickly shows how many times you should strum a chord in the bar before changing to a new chord, and is a quick way to show you which rhythms to play. Do take a moment to notice how the numbers on the tablature correspond with the fret numbers in the G Major chord diagram. There's one line for each string, and the fret number you should play is written directly onto the string.

This book comes with an audio download of every single example. If you're ever unsure how something should sound, then listen to the audio track and copy the rhythms and sounds you hear there. It's normally a lot easier to do this than to try to figure things out from the notation, especially if you don't read music. Don't worry, we'll cover all this in more detail as we go on!

Here's a reminder of what the diagrams below mean:

Diagram 1 shows you how to number the fingers of the fretting hand. If you are left handed, the same numbers apply to your right hand

Diagram 2 teaches you the notes on each of the open strings of the ukulele. Try to learn these, as it's always good to know a little bit about the instrument you're playing.

Diagram 3 shows how chords are notated on chord *grids*. Each dot is numbered and shows you which finger to place where.

Diagram 4 teaches you how the chord grid relates to where you place your fingers on the ukulele.

Diagram 5 shows how the chord will appear in standard musical notation and tablature (TAB for short). The TAB contains one line to represent each string and the frets you should play are shown by the numbers. Compare the tablature to the chord grid and see how they relate to one another.

Diagram 1

G C E A

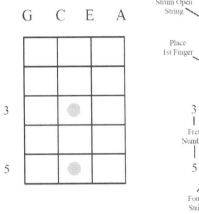

Diagram 2

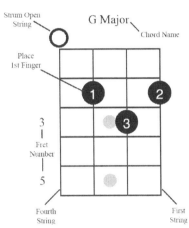

Diagram 3

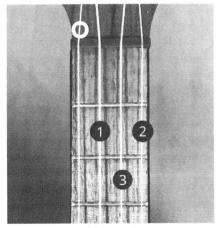

Diagram 4

Diagram 5

Chapter One: C Major and F Major

Let's get started by learning one of the easiest chords on the ukulele. C is one of the most common ukulele chords and you only need one finger to play it! The diagram below shows that you should place your third finger on the 3rd fret of the first string. If you're holding your ukulele as if you're about to play it, then the first string is the one closest to the floor.

Place the tip of your third finger just *behind* the fret and use just enough pressure to push the string against the fret to prevent it buzzing.

Hold down the chord and strum downwards slowly, playing one string at a time.

Listen out for any buzzing strings as this will mean that the underside of your finger is accidentally touching a string it shouldn't be. If you do hear buzzing, ensure you're using the very tip of your finger and that it doesn't touch any strings it shouldn't. Listen to the audio to hear how this should sound.

Example 1a

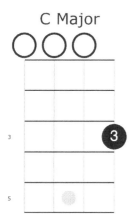

The next chord to learn is F Major. You'll need to use two fingers to hold down two notes on the neck.

Place your first and second fingers just behind the fret wire to play the notes shown on the first and second frets. Again, use just enough pressure to press the strings to the frets, then pluck each string individually. Listen out for any buzzes and adjust your hand position until they disappear. Be particularly careful with the open string between the two fretted notes as it's easy to accidentally brush it with the underside of your first finger.

Example 1b

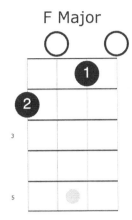

F Major

OK, great! We've learnt to play two different chords. The next step is to learn to switch between them while strumming. As I'm sure you know, this is the basis of every song in the world: strummed chords that change every few beats, played with a regular repeated rhythm.

I'd like you to play the next exercise with a metronome. You can download one for free onto your phone. Set the metronome to click at 60 beats per minute (bpm) and count out loud "1 2 3 4, 1 2 3 4" along with the click.

Hold down the C Major chord and strum it on beat "1". You now have four beats to move your fingers to the F Major chord and strum it on the next "1".

You might not be able to hold the C Major for the full four beats at first, because you need to leave yourself time to move your fingers, but as you improve you'll be able to keep it down for longer and longer, as the time it takes you to switch between chords reduces.

Keep switching between C and F for a few minutes and your dexterity will quickly increase.

Example 1c

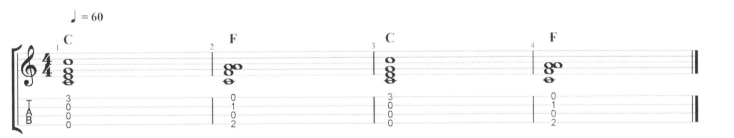

Now repeat this idea but strum a chord on *every beat*. Listen to the audio example to hear how this should sound. If you're just getting started, you may want to leave out the strum on beat four to give yourself time to change chords. Counting out loud 1 2 3 4 it would feel like this:

"strum, strum, strum (change chord), strum, strum, strum (change chord)."

Example 1d

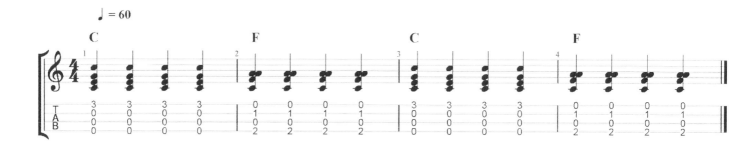

When you can move your fingers quickly and confidently between the C and F chords, try Example 1e. This chord sequence is similar to many songs including *Jambalaya* by Hank Williams.

Example 1e

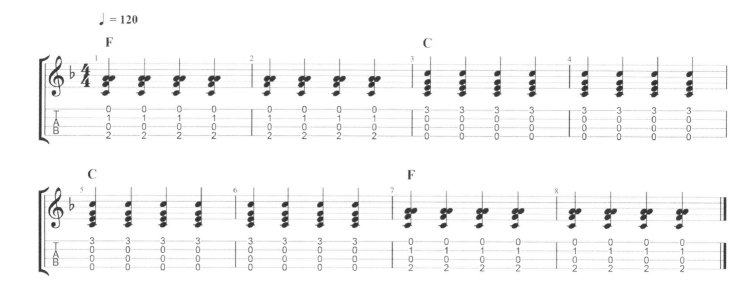

By changing this pattern slightly, you will end up with a chord pattern similar to *Achy Breaky Heart* by Billy Ray Cyrus. Notice that there are three bars of F Major followed one bar of C Major on the first line, then that pattern reverses on the second line. Music is normally organised into groups of four bars that form a musical "sentence".

Example 1f

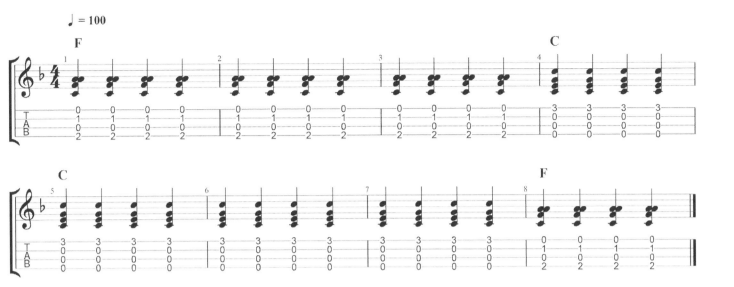

Not all music contains four beats in the bar. The next example has just three beats (strums) before changing chord. Try to *accent* the first chord in each bar, which means make it little louder with a slightly harder strum. You can count "ONE two three, ONE two three" along with your metronome to stay in time.

Example 1g

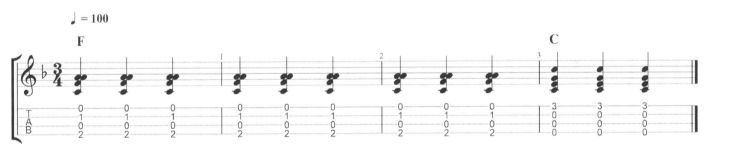

The next example is longer and combines the chords and rhythms you've learnt so far into song that you probably already know.

Go slowly and try to sing the lyrics, or hear them in your head, to help you stay in time and keep your place in the music. Also, look over the whole piece of music before you begin to play it, to get a feel for the rhythm (three strums per bar) and how often the chords change.

There are two patterns:

The first line contains three bars of F and one bar of C to make a four-bar phrase.

The second line switches between F and C every three strums.

Oh My Darling, Clementine

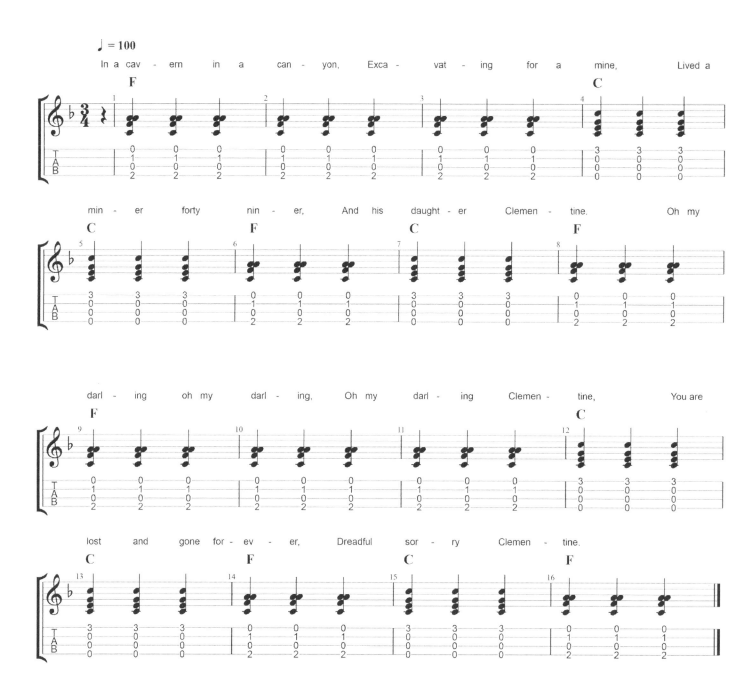

Chapter Two: Adding Rhythm

In the previous chapter we learnt a little about how rhythm on the ukulele is created by strumming the strings on every beat. In this section we're going to look at a few more strumming ideas that you can try on every single song you ever learn. Often, when you look for music, you'll just find a *chord chart* that tells you which chords are in the song, but it's up to you to bring the rhythm. By playing different rhythm patterns with your strumming hand (your right hand if you're right handed) you quickly add a lot of interest to the music. In fact, hundreds of songs use the same chords and it's the rhythm and melody that set them apart.

To learn rhythm, I want to show you how it is written in music, and how what's written relates to the pattern you strum on the ukulele.

First of all, we need to understand about bars and beats.

A bar is simply a *container* for the beats. An empty bar of music looks like this:

The 4/4 sign at the start is there to tell us that there are *four* beats in the bar. (Imagine the bar is a cake tin, and inside it is a cake cut into four quarters). If we fill the bar with *1/4 notes* it looks like this:

1/4 notes are really easy to play – in fact you've been playing them already!

Every time you see a 1/4 note (called a *crotchet* if you are in the UK) you play a down strum.

Down strums are always played on each beat, so if you're counting 1, 2, 3, 4 as in the previous chapter, each time you say a number you strum downwards. It helps a lot to stay in time if you tap your foot in time with the beat, so that your strumming hand, your foot, and even your whole body is moving in the same direction. This way you'll *feel* the beat, rather than needing to count it all the time.

Here is how this rhythm looks in ukulele tablature with a full chord in the notation. Notice the "n" symbols that indicate *down* strums.

Play each of the following chords with a down strum and play along with the audio track.

Example 2a

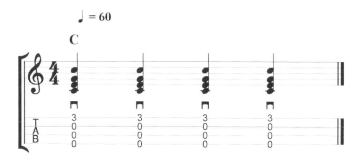

Now set your metronome to 60 bpm and play a down strum on each click while holding down the chord of C.

That's great, but it could get boring quite quickly. Let's make things a bit more interesting by adding more strums.

Imagine splitting each 1/4 note in half to give us *eight* notes in the bar. Unsurprisingly, these are called 1/8 or *eighth* notes.

Two 1/8th notes take the same amount of time to play as one 1/4 note, so all you need to do is squeeze in an up strum between each down strum. The up strums should be *exactly* midway between each down strum. The great news is that when you were playing 1/4 notes, your hand was coming up between each strum anyway. This time you just need to catch the strings with your fingers to add an 1/8th note strum.

On paper it looks like this:

Example 2b

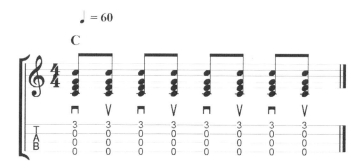

Notice the symbols to indicate *down* (n) and *up* (v) strums.

Set your metronome to 60 bpm and begin by playing just a down strum on each click. When you're ready, add up strums in between each down strum.

Count out loud:

"One and Two and Three and Four and"

You should be playing a down stum on each number and an up strum on every "and".

Fantastic! We've added in a lot of rhythm but it's quite "busy" and will quickly get boring.

Strumming rhythms on the ukulele gets much more interesting when we combine 1/4 notes and 1/8th notes for a bit of variety. These combinations are called *strumming patterns* and they add most of the rhythmic interest to your playing.

Let's combine 1/4 notes and 1/8th notes.

In Example 1e,

Beat 1 is a down strum

Beat 2 is a "down-up"

Beat 3 is a down strum

Beat 4 is a down strum

Before you play, set the metronome on 60 bpm and say out loud in time with the beat,

"One, Two and Three, Four" (Down, Down-Up, Down, Down).

Remember to tap your foot on the beats.

Repeat this with just your voice for a minute or two before adding the strums on the ukulele, while holding down a C or F chord.

Example 2c

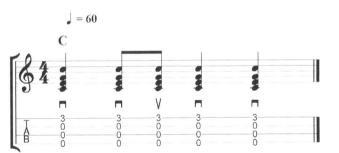

Saying the rhythm out loud really helps your brain to process what it needs to do to strum the rhythm in time.

When you're happy with the above, try the next idea with an F chord.

Repeat the following out loud and in time:

"One and Two, Three and Four" (Down-Up Down, Down-Up Down).

If it helps, you might want to think:

jin-gle bells, jin-gle bells

Listen to the audio before playing the following example! It's much easier to hear than it is to understand on paper.

Example 2d

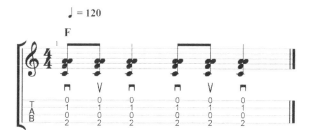

An important secret "life hack" for strumming is to realise that your strumming hand never stops moving and should lock in with the beat.

Remember that, *down strums are always on the beat* (the 1 2 3 4) and *up strums are always between the beats*. The hand never stops moving, so to create rhythms we either connect with the strings or we don't. It's a binary choice.

This physical action keeps you perfectly in time, like a little built-in conductor. To create rhythms, all we do is sometimes hit the strings and sometimes miss them. If you can tap your foot along with the beat, you'll find that your foot should always go down when your hand goes down.

Here are some other important rhythms to practice. Try them with the two chords we've learnt so far.

Down-Up, Down-Up, Down, Down

Example 2e

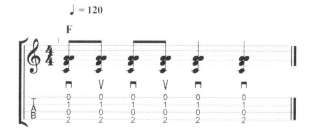

Down, Down, Down-Up, Down

Example 2f

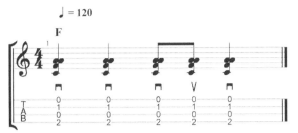

Remember to keep your strumming hand moving down and up *all the time*.

1/4 notes are played with a down strum. The 1/8th notes in between are played on the up strum.

If you don't want to play an 1/8th note, simply don't hit the strings on the way back up.

More Interesting Rhythms

We've covered some important rhythms that you'll use time and again in songs on the ukulele. Before we get back to learning more chords, I want to show you one more important rhythm that will add a ton of energy to your playing.

The easiest way to add more life to your strumming is to occasionally *miss out* strumming some of the down beats. To show you this idea, we need to introduce a new musical symbol: the 1/8th note *rest:*

A "rest" simply means *silence* or *don't strum*. It will always be written next to a strummed 1/8th note so that together they add up to one beat.

Take a look at Example 2k below.

Count out loud:

"One, Two, **Miss** and Four" (Down, Down, **Miss** Up, Down).

Hold down a C chord while you strum this rhythm. Keep the strumming hand moving all the time, but *miss* the strings on the down strum of beat 3, remembering to make contact again on the following up strum.

"Strum, Strum, Miss, Strum, Strum."

Listen to the audio before you play this to get a feel for how it should sound.

Example 2g

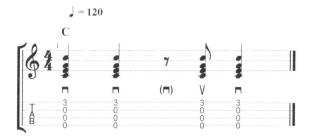

Once you have this idea sounding good, try the next rhythm.

*Down, Down Up, **Miss** Up, Down*

Example 2h

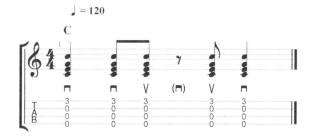

Finally, strum this.

*Down, **Miss** Up, **Miss** Up, Down.*

Example 2i

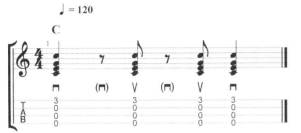

Now make up some of your own rhythms using the chords you know.

In the next chapter we'll get back to learning all the chords you need to become a great ukulele player, but I want you to remember that you can and should try any of the rhythms in this chapter on any later example. A catchy rhythm makes all the difference between an uninspiring chord sequence and an entertaining piece of music.

Chords give music harmony but strumming gives it rhythm. No one dances to a song's harmony, they dance to its rhythm. Keep that in mind because it's one of the secrets of music!

Chapter Three: The "Three-Chord Trick"

Another essential chord that you will find in lots of songs is G Major. Playing it requires you to use three fingers to play three different notes, all at the same time. Don't worry, you'll get the hang of it in no time!

To begin:

Put your first finger on the 2nd fret of the third string

Put your second finger on the 2nd fret of the first string (the one closest to the floor)

Finally, put your third finger on the 3rd fret of the second string.

Notice that the fingers make a kind of *triangle* shape. I found that remembering the finger shapes really helped me when I first started out, and you might too.

Once your fingertips are placed on the strings, pluck each one individually to check that the notes all sound clean and pure, and adjust your hand position if you need to. Now strum all four strings.

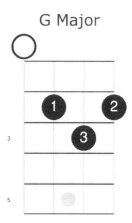

This next example combines G Major with the two chords you already know to create a chord pattern that sounds very familiar.

At first, you might want to play each chord just once before changing to the next, to help your fingers get used to the movements and become confident/automatic at moving between them. This is what we refer to as building *muscle memory*. Just like walking or writing, your body will quickly learn how to move without you having to think about firing every single muscle.

In the following example, the vertical lines with the dots at the start and end of the music are *repeat signs*. They indicate that the whole line should be repeated!

Example 3a

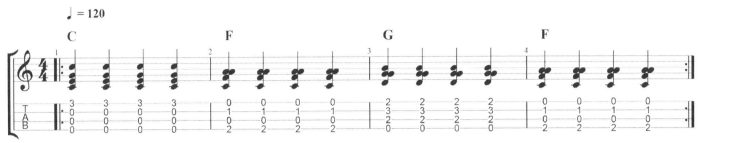

Next, play the same pattern again but this time with only two strums on each chord. It should sound very familiar because this sequence has been used in hundreds of songs (especially in the 1960s), including *Twist and Shout* by the Beatles, *Get Offa My Cloud* by the Rolling Stones, and many more.

Example 3b

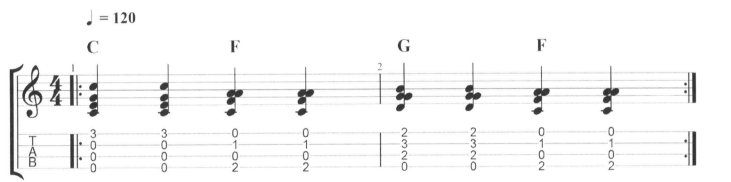

This chord pattern was often played using the rhythm in Example 3c.

Begin by counting:

"One, Two, Miss up, Four." (Down, Down, Miss-up, Down).

Once you can vocalise this rhythm confidently, have a go at strumming it.

Example 3c

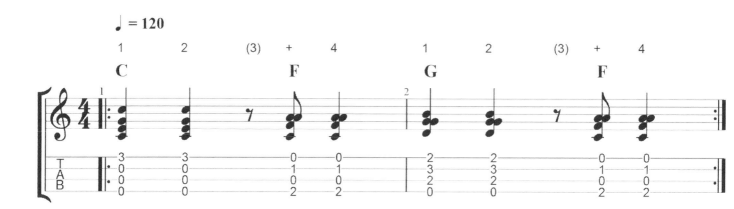

The next rhythm pattern is also very common.

Count:

"One, Two, Three, Miss-up" (Down, Down, Down, Miss-up).

Look at the end the first bar and you'll see that the final G Major chord on the up strum of beat four is *tied* to the G Major in the second bar.

These ties mean that you *play the first chord, but hold it for the length of the chord it's tied to.* You do *not* strum the chord in the second bar, you simply let the final strum in the first bar ring out for the whole of the second bar.

This sounds great, but also gives you plenty of time to get the fingers in the right place to start again! If you're not sure of the rhythm, listen to the audio track and you'll quickly get the hang of it. If you've not already done so, remember that you can download the audio to your computer from **www.fundamental-changes.com**.

This pattern sounds similar to the song *La Bamba*.

Example 3d

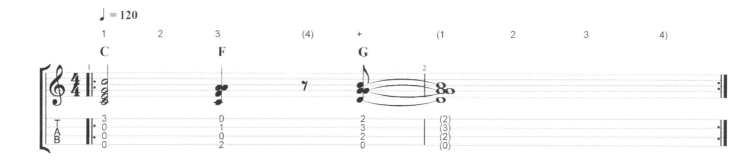

Now let's learn a longer song that uses three chords.

I've written it out with one strum on each beat, but once you've learnt it like that, try playing any of the rhythms you've learnt in the previous two chapters.

Man of Constant Sorrow

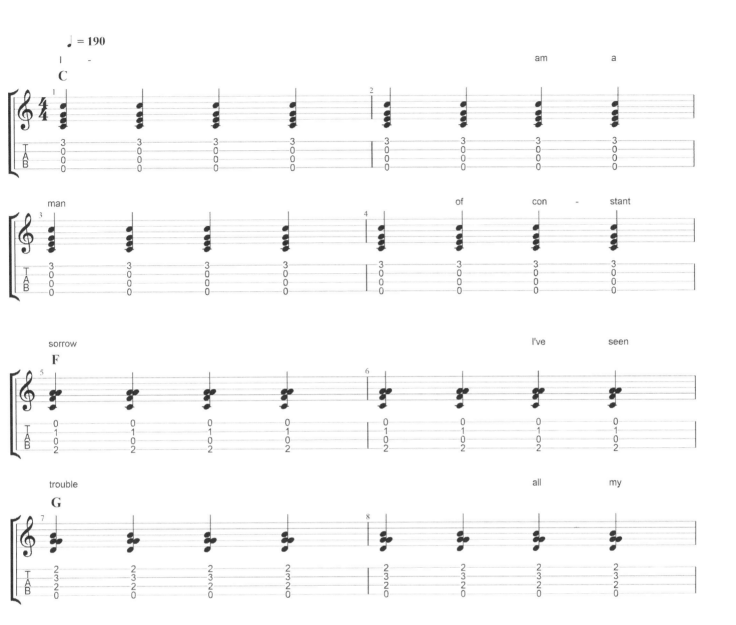

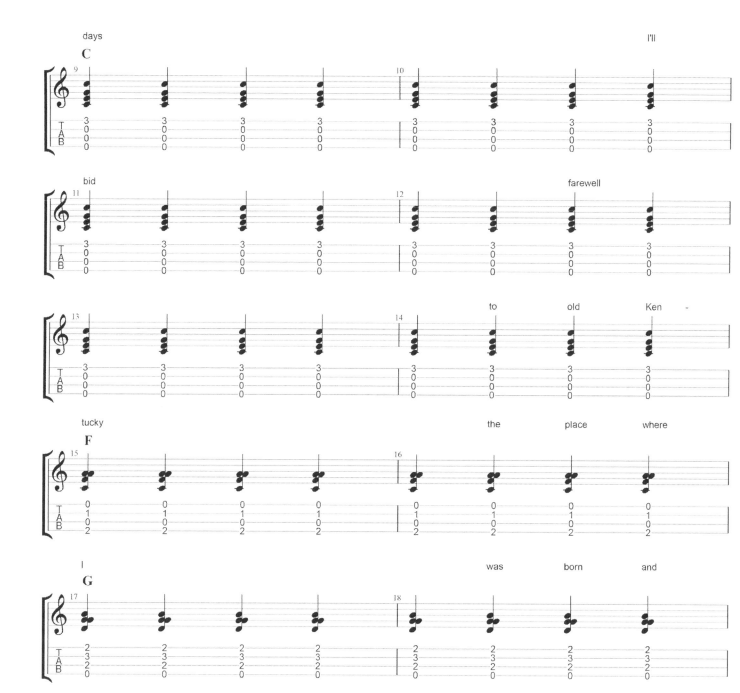

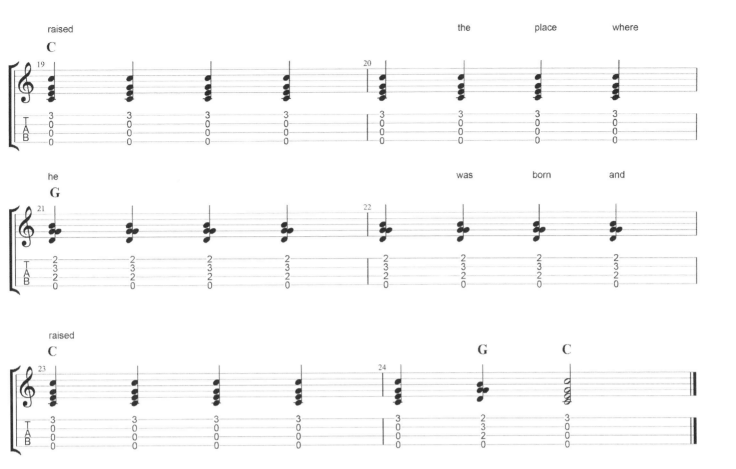

Chapter Four: C, G, Am and F

In this chapter we're going to learn a very important chord sequence. In fact, it's probably the most common progression in all pop music, with literally thousands of songs being written using it. First though, we need to learn another essential chord: A Minor (often written as just "Am").

The A minor chord can be played with just one finger! Simply place your second finger on the 2nd fret of the fourth string. As always, pick the strings separately at first to check that all the notes sound clear, then give it a strum.

Example 4a

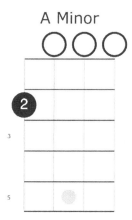

When we add Am to the three chords we already know, we can play this iconic chord pattern used in thousands of songs.

Have a go at playing Example 4b. You will notice that it sounds incredibly familiar!

You'll hear this sequence in famous songs like *With or Without You* by U2, *Wherever You Will Go* by The Calling, *Country Roads* by John Denver and *Someone Like You* by Adele, to name a few.

It really is a great sequence to learn, not to mention fun and satisfying to play something so instantly recognisable.

Example 4b

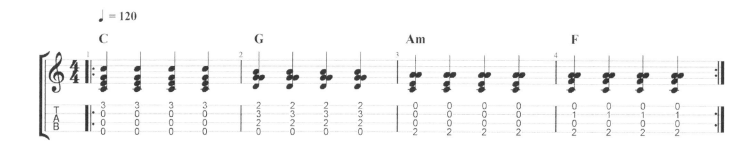

Changing smoothly between four chords might seem like a big step, so here are some tips to help you learn *any* new chord sequence.

- Place your fingers in the correct position for the first chord you want to play.

- Pick through the notes individually at first to make sure that each note in the chord sounds clear.

- Are there notes that are buzzing or muted? If so, check that the *tip* of the fingers are pressed against the string firmly enough, just *behind* the fret wire, not on the wire itself. Check that your fretting finger isn't accidently touching an adjacent string and stopping it from sounding.

- Strum the strings to hear the full chord.

- Repeat the previous steps with the next chord.

- When all of the chords sound good, set your metronome to click at 60 bpm and strum each chord, holding it for *two* beats. Allow yourself the next two beats to change to the next chord in the sequence.

- Next, strum each chord on the first three 1/4 notes strums and change to the next chord on beat four.

- When you can change between all four chords confidently and in time, strum each one on each of the four 1/4 notes in the bar and change chords in the gap between the fourth beat of the first bar and the first beat of the next.

- Add in some 1/8th notes by strumming Down, Down, Down up, Down.

- Add in some more 1/8th notes by strumming Down, Down up, Down up, Down.

- Finally, add a bit more energy by missing out some of the down beats. Begin with the strumming pattern Down, Down, Miss-Up, Down, then try the other patterns in the second half of Chapter Two.

Remember to always play along with a metronome, tap your foot and count the rhythm out loud if you can.

Now, let's look at another rhythm pattern you can try with this chord sequence.

If you play the same thing, but with just two strums on each chord, you create a pattern like the one used in *Let It Be* by the Beatles, *No Woman No Cry* by Bob Marley, and many other songs.

Example 4c

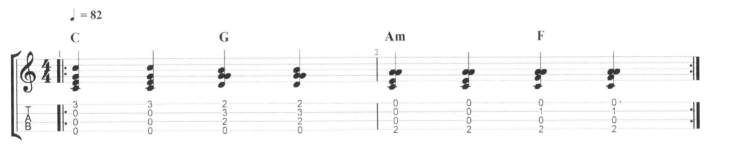

Let's swap the order of the chords to Am, F, C, then G.

As with any new chord pattern, begin by changing very slowly at first. You might want to play just one strum on each chord and hold it for four beats before switching, until you can change smoothly as described earlier.

This sequence will probably sound as familiar as the first pattern!

These chords are used in songs like *Save Tonight* by Eagle Eye Cherry, *One of Us* by Joan Osbourne, *Zombie* by the Cranberries, and the chorus of *Africa* by Toto.

Example 4d

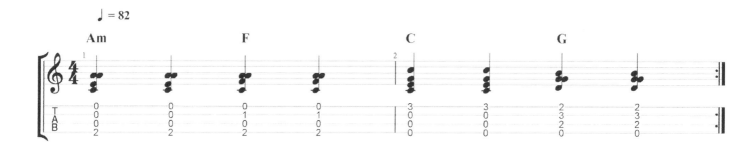

If we change the order of the chords again to F, C, G, Am, we create a pattern that sounds a bit like *Higher Love* by Steve Winwood.

Try this rhythmic variation, strumming only on beat one and the "and" after beat two.

Notice the tie lines joining the "and" of beat two with the chord on beat three. As before, this means that you play the first strum on the C chord and *hold it for the value of the chord it's tied to,* so there are only two strums in each bar. Again, listen to the audio track if you're unsure – it's much easier to hear these rhythms than read them off the paper.

Count:

*"**One**, Miss **and**, Three, Four"*

Strum only on the beats written in bold.

Example 4e

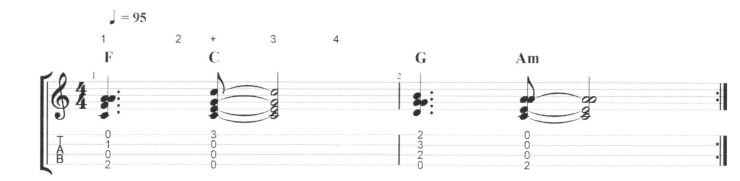

Finally, let's switch the chords around once more to C, Am, F, G, and we'll create a common chord pattern from the 1950s that is also similar to Ed Sheeran's *Perfect*. Strum four times on each chord.

Example 4f

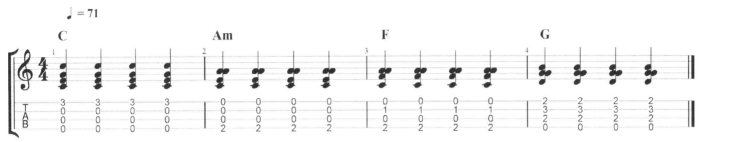

Now add the strumming pattern from Example 4e…

*"**One**, Two **and**, Three, Four"*

…and you'll create something that sounds a little bit like *Stand by Me* by Ben E. King.

Example 4g

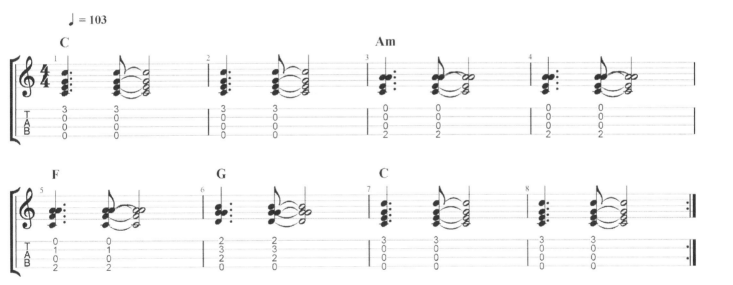

Now, have a go at playing and singing a longer song using what you've learnt so far.

Go Lassie Go

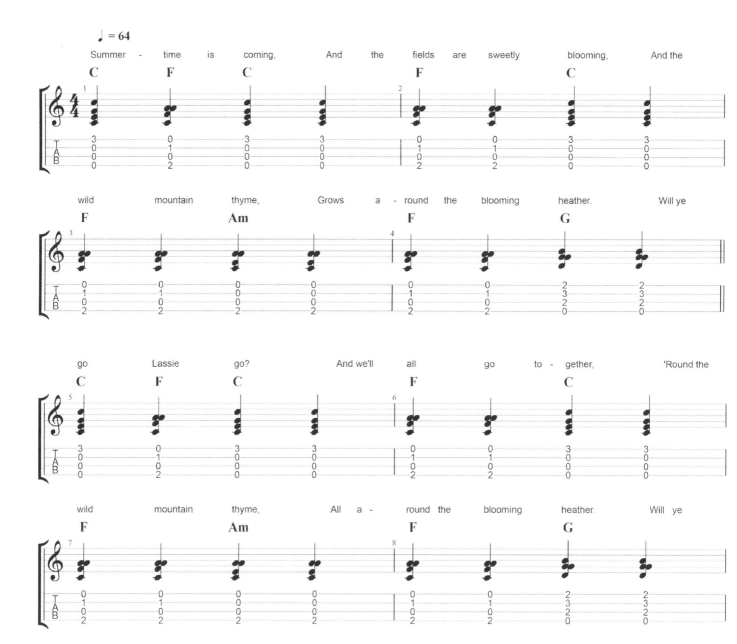

Chapter Five: Introducing D Major

Let's learn another very useful chord: D Major. Notice how all three fingers are placed on the 2nd fret. This might feel like a bit of a squeeze at first, and you'll need to make sure that the underside of the third finger doesn't touch the open string and stop it from ringing. Make sure it's only the tips of the fingers touching the strings and that they're pointing directly through the neck.

Example 5a

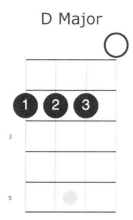

Added D Major to the chords we already know this unlocks lots of new songs.

In fact, you can now play the "three-chord-trick" from Chapter Three in the key of G Major (G, C and D) which is very common on ukulele.

Practise using the D chord in this chord sequence. Learn it by first strumming each chord for two beats before playing the pattern in the example below.

"**One**, **Two**, Three **and Four**" (**Down**, **Down**, Miss-**up**, **Down**).

Example 5b

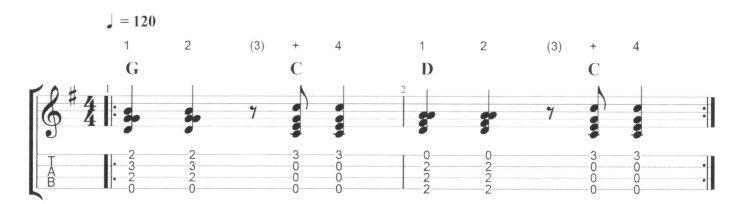

The chords G, D and Am are used in *Knocking on Heaven's Door* by Bob Dylan and *Rise* by Gabrielle, along with hundreds of others.

The transition from D to Am is nice and smooth, you just have to remove the second and third fingers.

Example 5c

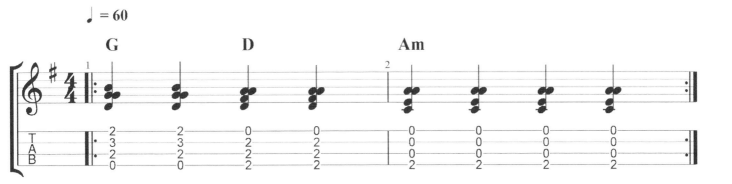

We can add to this to create a chord sequence similar to the verse from *With a Little Help From my Friends* by The Beatles.

If you want to make your chords sound a bit punchier, try relaxing the pressure of your fretting fingers just after each strum. Not enough so that they come off the strings – you want to keep them in contact with the strings at all times – but just enough so that the chord is deadened instead of ringing.

Notice how this makes the chords sound more detached from each other on the audio track.

Example 5d

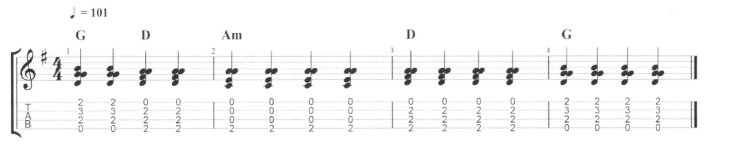

If you switch the order of these chords around to G, Am, C, D, you create a pattern like the one in *Love is All Around* by The Trogs or *Back for Good* by Take That.

Once you can play the basic strumming pattern below, why not try strumming some rhythms of your own? Borrow ideas from the previous examples or try something completely different!

Example 5e

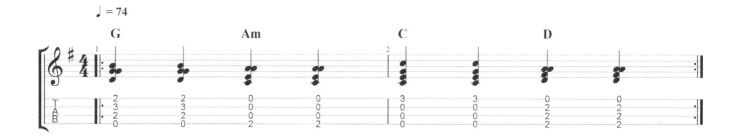

Finally, here are the chords for a classic old Hawaiian song almost always played on the ukulele: *Aloha Oe*.

It also requires you to play a C7 chord, but don't worry it's very easy. It's just like the C Major chord but with the finger on the 1st fret instead of the 3rd.

Example 5f

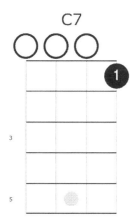

Aloha Oe

Chapter Six: Introducing E7

Now we are going to learn another *dominant 7th* chord. This type of chord has a slightly tense sound and normally wants to *resolve* that *tension* to another chord.

Below is a chord grid for E dominant 7th. When writing it, we shorten the name to E7. It is often seen just before the chord Am.

Example 6a

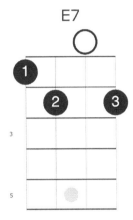

The next chord sequence is similar to *Delilah* by Tom Jones and will teach you to change from Am to E7.

Play each chord with just one strum on each chord until your fingers get familiar with the change. E7 can be a tricky chord at first, so be sure to use the steps in Chapter Four that teach you how to practise new chords.

Example 6b

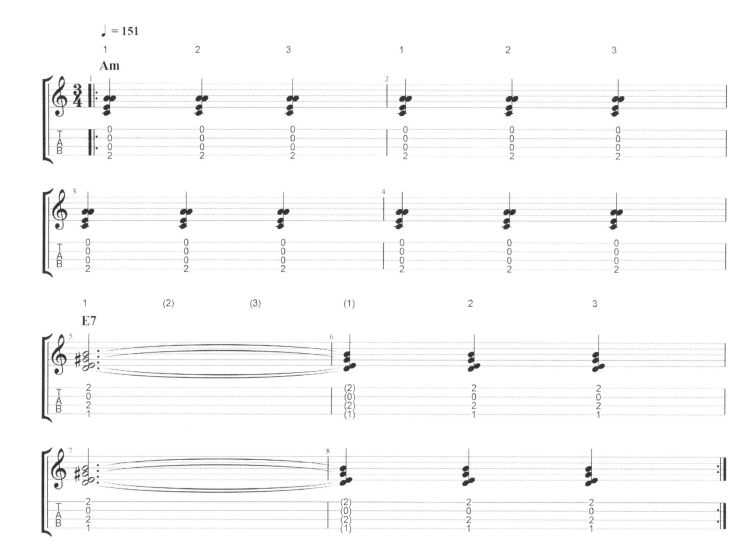

Let's add in an F chord before the change to E7 to make the sequence Am, Am, F, E7. This is a chord pattern used lots in pop and rock music. You can hear it in songs like *Sweet Dreams* by the Eurythmics and it's also the basis of the guitar riff to *Seven Nation Army* by the White Stripes.

Isolate and learn the change from F to E7 initially, before playing the full pattern.

Example 6c

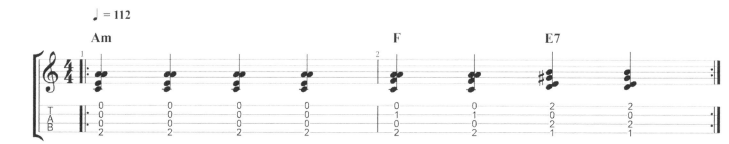

If we add the chords F and G, we create one of the most common sequences of all time. Similar to the chords used in *Hit the Road Jack*, this require lots of jumping around on the fretboard, so make sure you go slow and use the steps from Chapter Four to help you master the music accurately.

Once you have the chords down, play the pattern at around 60 bpm at first and work up the speed gradually. When you're ready, add some more interesting rhythms to your strums.

Example 6d

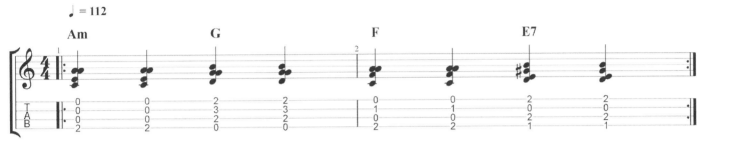

Notice how the E7 chord creates a *pull* back to Am and doesn't feel finished until it is resolved.

Here is another good example of this tension, similar to the one used in *The Passenger* by Iggy Pop.

Example 6e

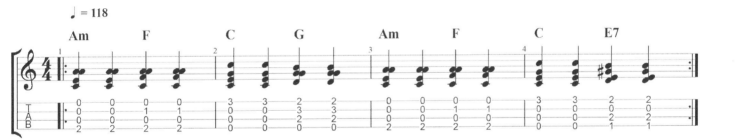

Now you are really getting to grips with these chords!

Add in a D chord and you can play something similar to *House of The Rising Sun*.

Example 6f

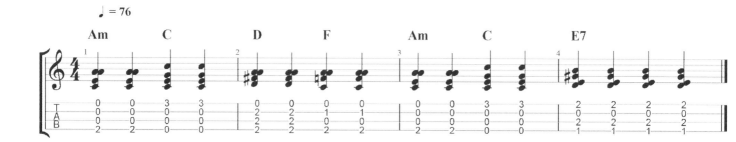

Now you can put together everything you have been doing so far and have a go at *Scarborough Fair*.

Scarborough Fair

Chapter Seven: Introducing A Major

Here's how you play A Major:

Example 7a

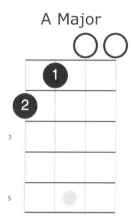

Combining this with the chords you already know will open up many new song possibilities including chord sequences similar to the one used in *Fly Away* by Lenny Kravitz.

Example 7b

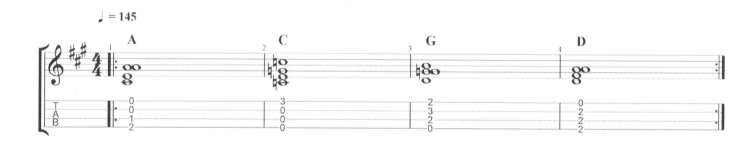

When you can switch between the chords smoothly, try them with the following *down, up, down, up* strumming motion shown below.

Notice the rest on beat four? This is a *1/4 note rest* and lasts for one beat, so you must be completely silent on beat 4. Count:

"One and Two and Three, **Rest**" (Down-up, Down-up, Down, **Miss**)

As always, listen to the audio to hear how this should sound. It's a much more musical way to learn rhythm!

Example 7c

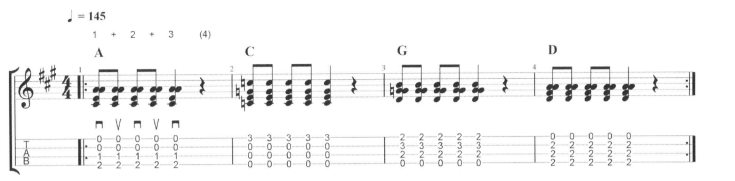

Notice how this strumming pattern really brings the chords to life.

Another important feel is to only play chords on certain beats or to add accents to particular strums.

This next patten is very common in Reggae and Ska music, and involves only playing chords on beats 2 and 4. You'll miss out the strums on beats 1 and 3, which can take a bit of getting used to. Counting out loud and tapping your foot will help a lot.

This pattern sounds similar to *Stir it Up* by Bob Marley. Strum *only* on beats **two** and **four**. Count:

"One, **Two**, Three, **Four**" (Miss, **Strum**, Miss, **Strum**)

As always, check out the audio and play with a metronome.

Example 7d

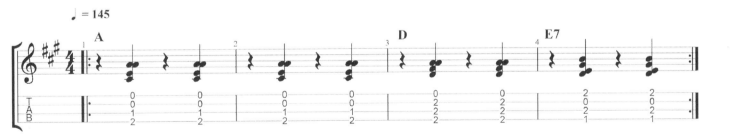

A similar, but more energetic rhythm pattern is to play in 1/8th notes but only strum on the "and" of the beat. In other words, you only strike the strings on an up strum.

This will create an upbeat, bouncy feel, similar to Ska classics such as *A Message to You Rudy* by The Specials. Count:

"One **and**, Two **and**, Three **and**, Four **and**" (Miss-up, Miss-**up**, Miss-**up**, Miss-**up**).

Top Tip: Mime the first down strum on the beat but miss the strings. Catch them on the way up with your hand and repeat the pattern. Again, it's important to listen to the audio track so you get this tricky feel correct.

Example 7e

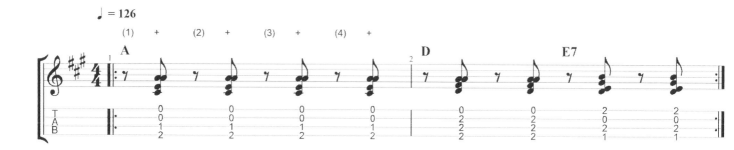

You can also add interest to a chord pattern by playing rhythms that are held *across* beats. This is called *syncopation*.

In the next rhythm pattern, even though you don't strum on beat 3, notice the *ghost* strum in brackets.

Strum across the strings without hitting them to help you keep the timing on this tricky rhythm. As always, use the audio to ensure you reproduce it accurately.

For the first bar, count:

"One, Two and, Three **and, Four"** (**Down, Down-up**, Miss-**up**, **Down**).

Example 7f

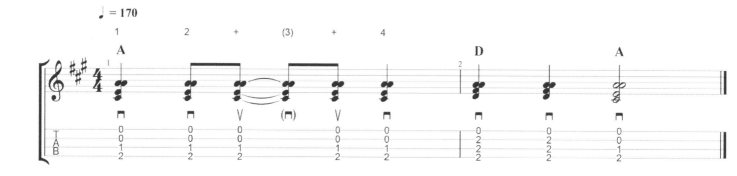

Now try the song *Keep On The Sunny Side* and feel free to experiment by adding your own syncopated strumming ideas.

Keep On The Sunny Side

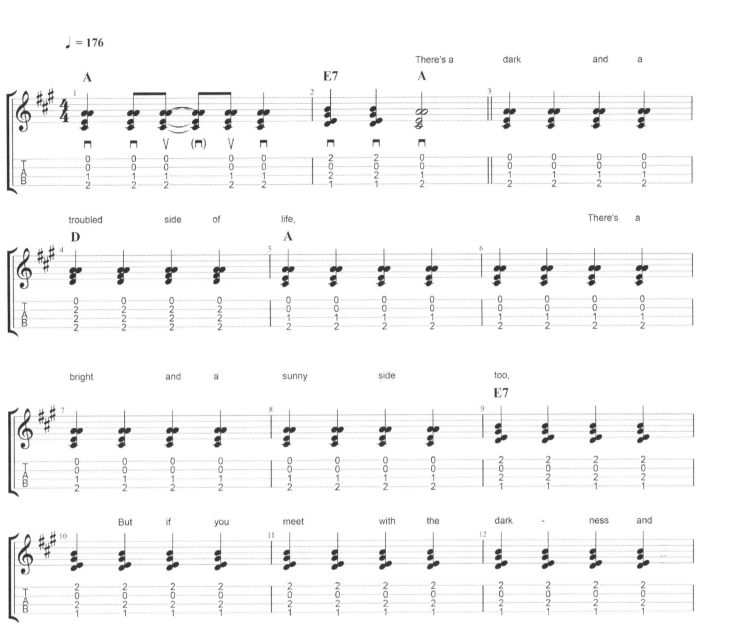

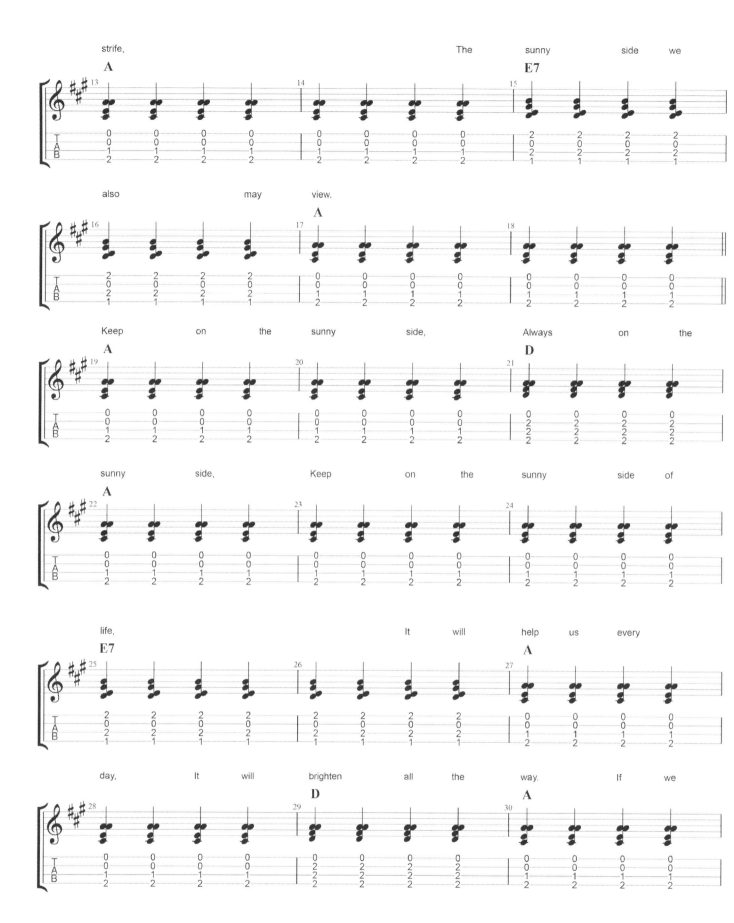

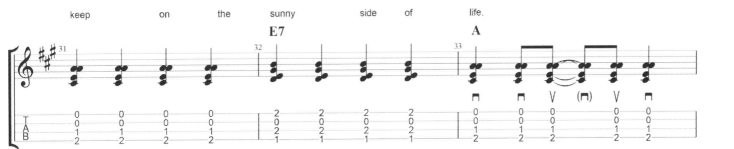

Chapter Eight: Dominant 7th Chords and The Blues

You already know C7 and E7, but two more useful 7th chords are A7 and D7.

Example 8a

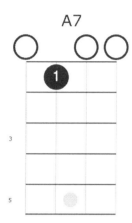

Example 8b

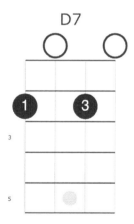

Dominant 7 chords are often used in Blues music.

With A7, D7 and E7, we can play a chord form known as the *Twelve-bar Blues*.

The twelve-bar blues is used in countless songs, many of which are Rock 'n' Roll classics: *Johnny B. Goode* by Chuck Berry, *Hound Dog* by Elvis, *Tutti Fruiti* by Little Richard, and *Rock Around the Clock* by Bill Haley. It's also been used in songs like *Rock and Roll* by Led Zeppelin and *Gimme One Reason* by Tracey Chapman.

The dominant 7th chords add a real bluesy texture and colour to the sequence.

Example 8c

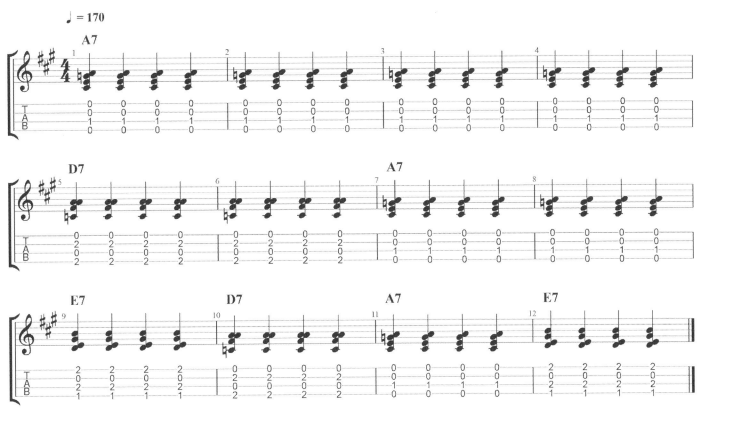

That's fine, of course, but strumming the same chords for such a long time can get a little boring. A great way to make the twelve-bar blues more interesting is to use a *riff* (a repeating musical rhythmic phrase) instead of strumming a static A7 chord.

In the next example, pay attention to how the note on the second string of the ukulele moves from the open string, to the 2nd fret, to the 3rd fret, and then back on each beat. It's quite easy to play too, because you can simply hold the A7 chord with your first and second fingers and use your third and fourth fingers to play the fretted notes on the second string.

Example 8d

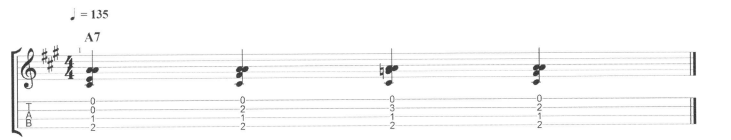

This *riff* is actually made from three separate chord shapes: A, A6 and a different fingering of A7.

Practise each chord separately at first and change between them slowly while gradually building speed. Notice that you only need to change one finger at a time to go between them!

Example 8e

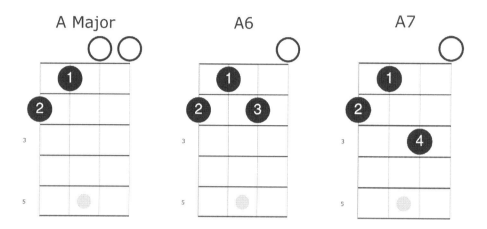

Once you have mastered the riff in A, play this riff instead of the static D7 chord in bars five and six. Again, you can hold the D7 chord with three fingers then use your spare finger to play the melody – this time on the first string. Notice how the melody on the first string is played on frets 0, 2, 3, then 2 again, and the note changes on every beat.

Example 8f

This pattern can be shown as three chord shapes: D, D6 and an alternative fingering of D7.

This could be a little tricky at first, because you need to use all four fingers at certain points during the riff.

If you have trouble, be sure to use the trusty *Steps for practising a new chord pattern* from Chapter Four!

Example 8g

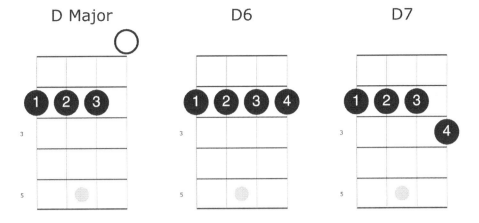

D Major   D6   D7

Now combine the riffs on A7 and D7 and add them into the full twelve-bar blues. The E7 chord doesn't have any alterations, so you can just strum it for four beats when it appears.

Example 8h

Remember to add other rhythms to the twelve-bar blues. You don't have to play a riff every time – a syncopated strumming pattern works wonders. There are thousands of twelve-bar blues songs to choose from, so take a quick look on Google and you will be sure to find some you know!

To finish up this chapter, let's play and sing a whole song that uses some of these dominant 7th chords.

Amazing Grace

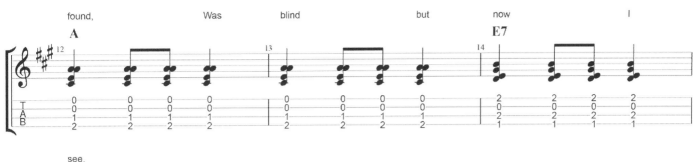

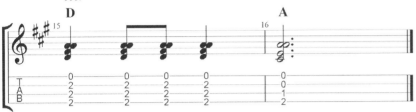

Chapter Nine: More Minor Chords

You already know one minor chord, Am. Here are two more that come up all the time on ukulele: Dm and Em.

Example 9a

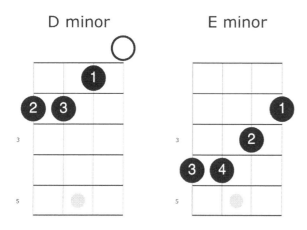

Em might feel a bit stretchy at first, as it uses all four fingers and is a little higher on the fretboard than the other chords we've studied.

Learn Em by switching from to it from other chords you already know. It will sound great next to Am, G, D7 and C.

When you can move between Em and other chords smoothly, try it in this chord progression similar to *Yellow Submarine* by the Beatles.

Example 9b

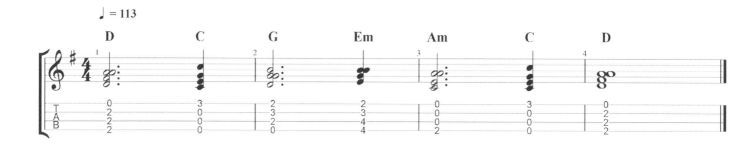

Now learn Dm in the same way. It'll sound great next to A, G, C and F.

When you're confident you can form it quickly and cleanly, play it in this sequence that's reminiscent of *Can't Help Falling in Love*.

Example 9c

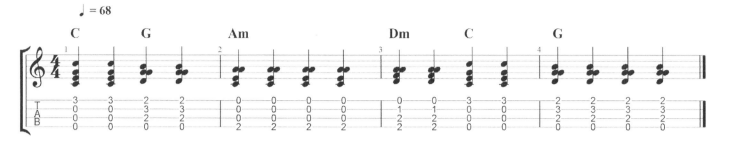

If you combine both Em and Dm, you can create a chord pattern similar to *What a Wonderful World*.

Example 9d

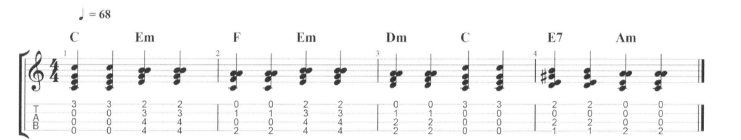

Here is a chord pattern similar to *Killing Me Softly*.

Start by playing just one strum on each chord, then experiment with some of your own rhythms when you're confident that you can change chords perfectly with the metronome set on 60bpm (beats per minute). You can always speed up later.

Example 9e

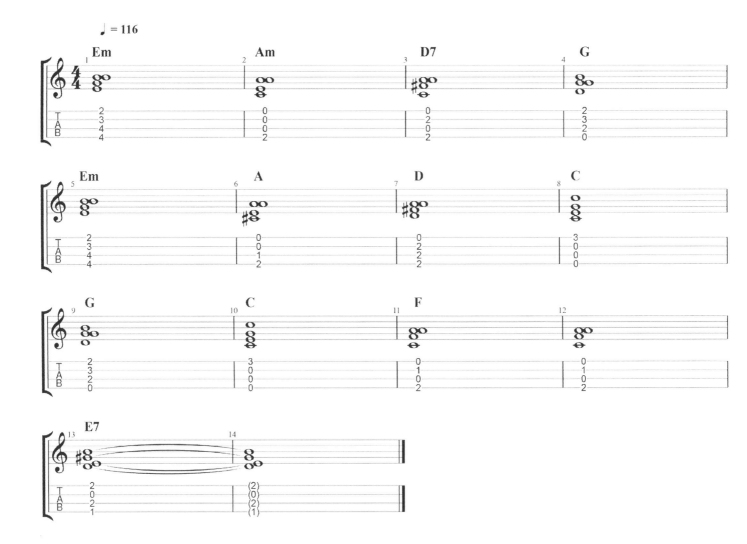

Example 9f uses these chords in a sequence similar to *Ain't No Sunshine*.

Example 9f

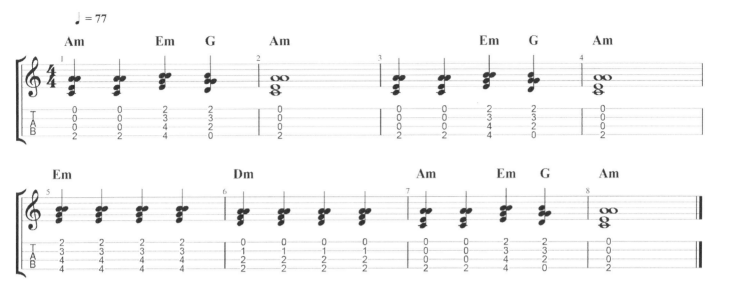

Once you get to grips with these new minor chords, try picking each string individually instead of strumming them all at the same time. This *fingerpicking* can really make your chord pattern come to life!

First, pick the fourth string (the one closest to you) with your thumb (labelled *p*)

Pick the third string with your index finger (*i*)

Pick the second string with your middle finger (*m*)

Pick the first string with your ring finger (*a*)

Then reverse the pattern to return back to the fourth string and start again. Try it with the Am chord below and make sure you listen to the audio track to hear how it should sound.

Example 9g

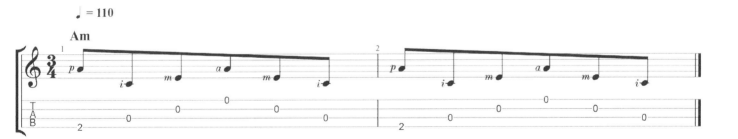

Once you can play the picking pattern, try using it on some of the other chord progressions you have learnt, like *What a Wonderful World* and *Scarborough Fair*.

Now let's combine many of the different chords you've learnt so far into a classic song that's been covered by countless great artists: *Nobody Knows You When You're Down and Out.*

Nobody Knows You When You're Down and Out

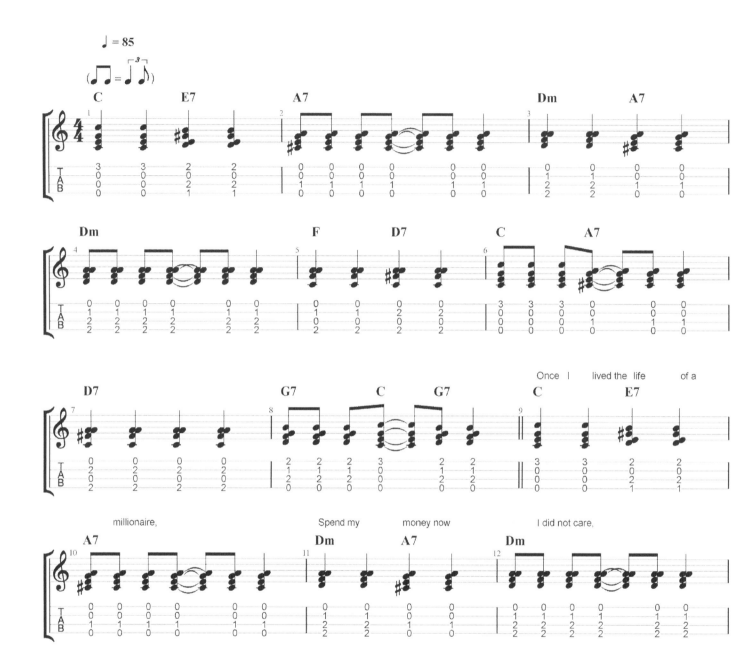

Chapter Ten: Moveable Chords

Any chord shape that doesn't contain any open strings can be moved up and down the neck.

This means that you can slide the entire shape up or down the neck to the desired note to play another chord of the same *quality* (Major, Minor, 7 etc).

You have already learnt one moveable shape: Em.

E minor

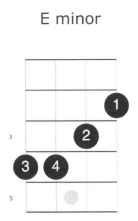

Em doesn't contain any open strings, so if you slide it up one fret it becomes Fm. If you slide it up two frets it becomes F#m (pronounced "F sharp minor").

Example 10a

F minor   F# minor

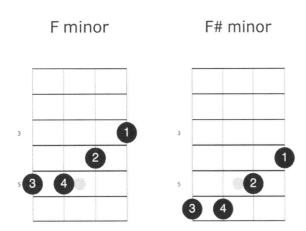

A *barre* chord is another very useful way to play a moveable chord shape and an important minor barre chord shape is Bm.

A barre chord uses one finger to create a "bar" across multiple strings.

Barre chords are all movable because they don't contain any open strings, so it is possible to slide a barred shape up and down the strings to play different chords.

Sliding chord shapes up and down the neck only works if they don't contain any open strings. Here's why:

Play an A minor chord, then slide your fingers up one fret and strum the chord again.

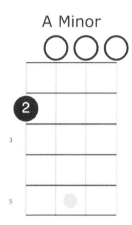

A Minor

It sounds wrong because you moved the one fretted note up the neck, but the notes on the open strings stayed put. If we could *bring* the open string with us when we moved the chord up the neck, we could keep the relationship between all the notes the same and not leave any notes behind.

Barre chords allow us to bring the open strings with us as we move chord shapes around the neck. Bm is the same *shape* as Am, because by placing the index finger across the strings we bring the open strings up the neck with us to the correct pitch.

Example 10b

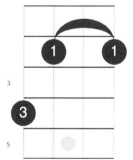

B minor

If you move the barre up to the 3rd fret you create Cm. If you move one fret down, you create Bbm ("B flat minor").

To play this Bm barre chord, you bar the first finger across the strings as shown here:

Example 10c

These barre chords are very useful for a couple of reasons.

Firstly, if you know the notes on the ukulele neck you can quickly play any chord you like, as long as you know its barre chord shape.

Secondly, *chromatic* chord movements (moving one fret up or down between chords) suddenly become possible. Check out the idea below. Listen to the audio first and you'll hear how cool this movement sounds.

Example 10d

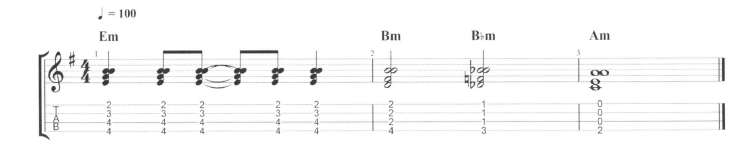

Barre chords let us play chord progressions like this one, similar to *Jamming* by Bob Marley. Watch out for the syncopation and remember to count the rhythm out loud before playing it.

Example 10e

Barre chords are also used in this sequence that's similar to *Hey There Delilah* by The Plain White Ts.

The jump from D to F#m is a big one, so isolate that change and build up speed gradually.

Example 10f

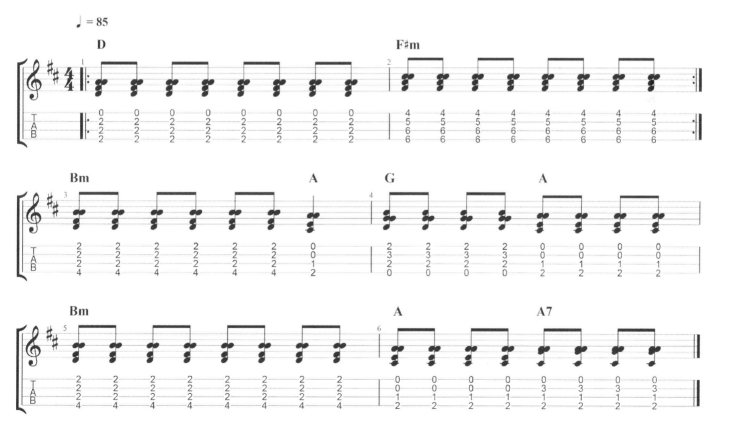

Another useful moveable chord that pops up frequently is E Major (E).

Example 10g

E major

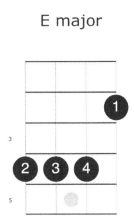

Here's a funky rhythm that incorporates all these moveable shapes and is a similar progression to *Get Lucky* by Daft Punk.

Watch out for the strum played slightly after beat 2. This 1/16th note (*semi-quaver*) delay helps give the pattern its groove.

Use the audio to make sure the timing is accurate and try to copy my feel.

Example 10h

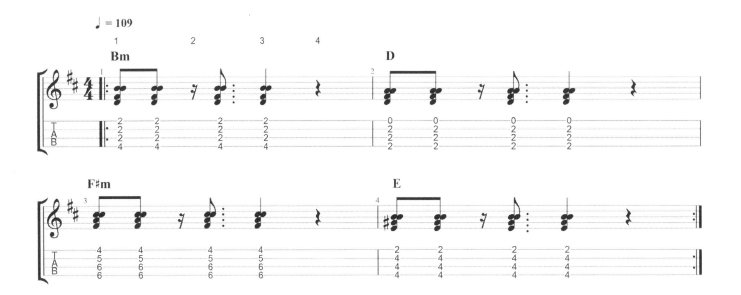

One final moveable chord shape for this chapter is Bb Major. To play this quickly, finger the Bb *minor* shape and simply place your second finger on the third string at the 2nd fret.

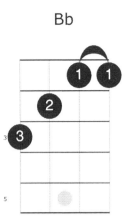

Bb

This addition to your list of moveable shapes gives you a really comprehensive range of major and minor chord voicings and makes most popular songs possible. Try this sequence, similar to *Yesterday* by the Beatles.

Example 10i

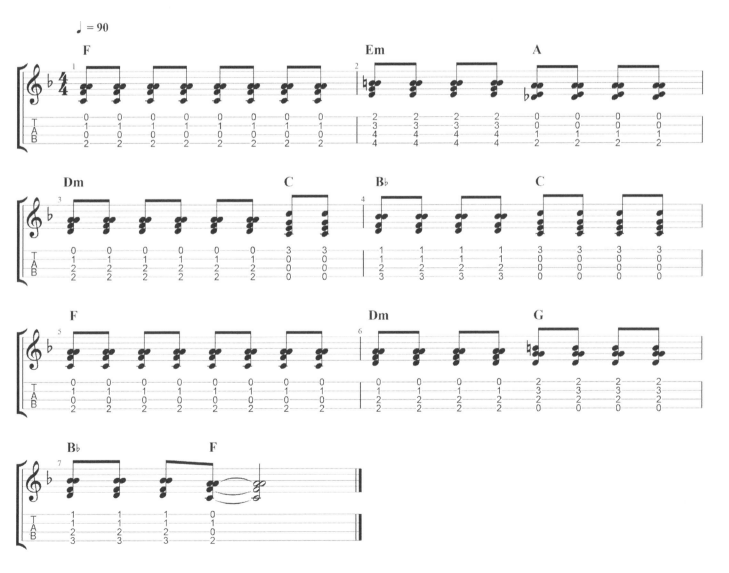

This sequence is similar to *Sittin' on the Dock of the Bay* by Otis Redding.

Example 10j

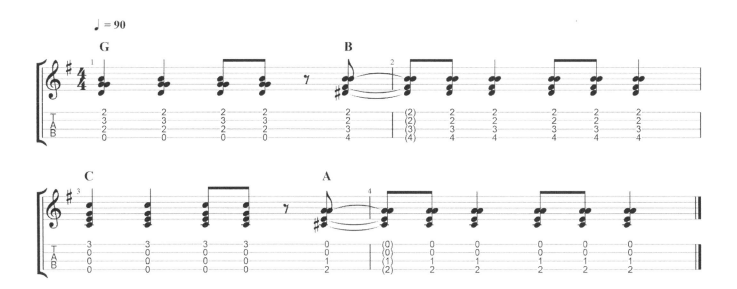

To end this chapter, here's a new picking pattern that you can use on any chord progression.

Hold the chord shape down for the entire bar, but start by picking just the single note on the third string. When you've picked that, strum the full chord. This picking pattern works especially well on ballads and slow tempo songs like *Yesterday*.

Example 10k

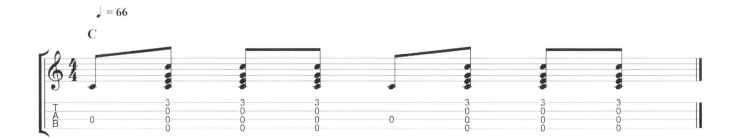

Once you have it sounding smooth and clear, try singing and playing *Danny Boy*.

Danny Boy

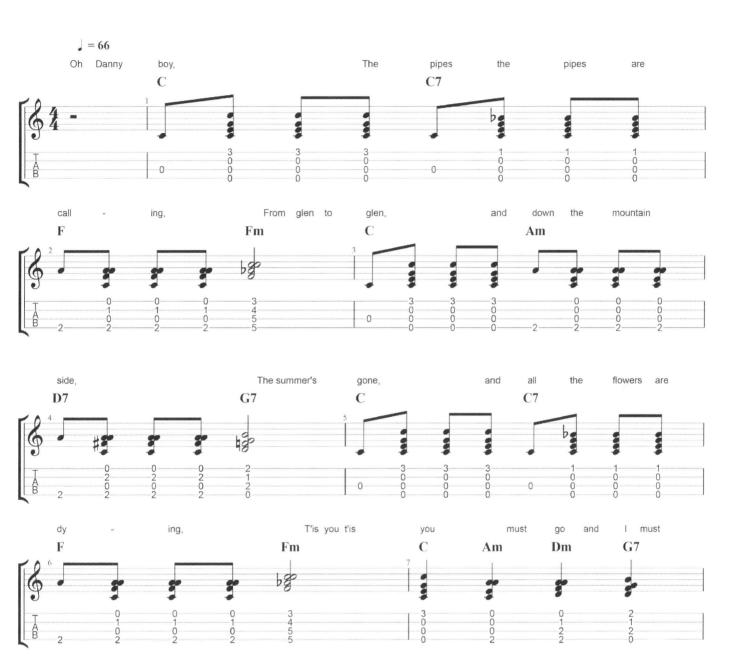

Chapter Eleven: Moveable 7ths and Minor 7ths

You already know some different 7 chords, such as E7, A7 and D7, but none of them are moveable.

The next chord you'll learn is a movable voicing of F#7.

Notice that it is very similar to E7, but it's been moved up two frets, and the open string has been replaced with a fretted note.

As it is a movable shape, it can be played anywhere on the neck to create different 7 chords. For example, it can be played one fret higher as an alternative fingering of a G7 chord, or one fret lower to make F7.

Example 11a

F#7

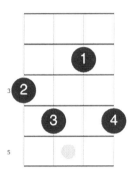

It's worth mentioning that F#7 is the exact same chord as Gb7. Many notes in music have more than one name and these notes are called *enharmonic*.

C# = Db

D# = Eb

F# = Gb

A# = Bb

This F#7 chord shape will help you unlock chord progressions like the one below, which is similar to *Hotel California*. Before you try it, get confident changing in and out of F#7 by repeatedly switching between it and the Bm barre chord. Make sure you play along with a metronome.

B minor   F#7

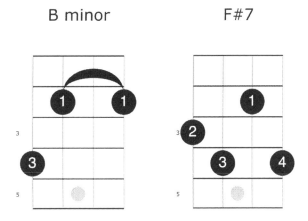

The *dotted* 1/4 note rhythm shown in the example below is a very common rhythm pattern and should be counted like this:

"**One,** Two **and**, Three, Four" (**Down,** Miss-**up**, Miss, Miss).

As always, listen to the audio before playing the example and you'll pick it up in no time at all.

Example 11b

You can use F#7 in this chord sequence that's similar to *Wake Me Up* by Avici

Notice how F#7 wants to *resolve* to Bm, just E7 wants to resolve to Am.

The rhythm below uses 1/16th notes, so be sure to check it out on the audio track first, and keep your strumming hand moving up and down four times per beat, whether you make contact with the strings or not.

Count:

"**1** e & a, **2** e & a, **3** e & a, **4** e & a"

Example 11c

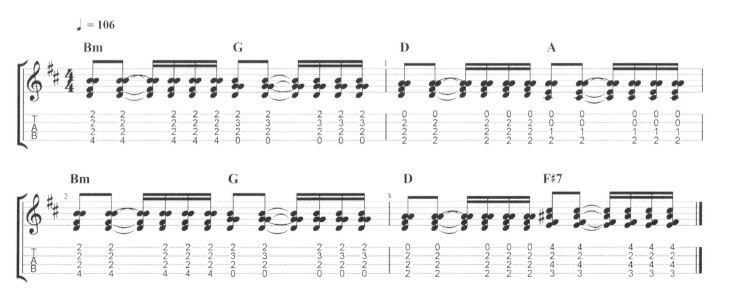

Here is another useful 7 barre chord voicing.

Example 11d

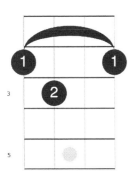

B7

Notice that it is the same *shape* as A7, but the barre with the first finger across the 2nd fret makes it moveable. You could go up one fret to play C7 or down one fret to play Bb7.

B7 appears in many famous chord sequences, like *Creep* by Radiohead.

Here is a similar pattern with a really nice 1/16th note strumming pattern that you can easily transfer to other chord progressions.

Count:

"**1** e & a, **2** e & a, **3** e & a, **4** e & a"

Example 11e

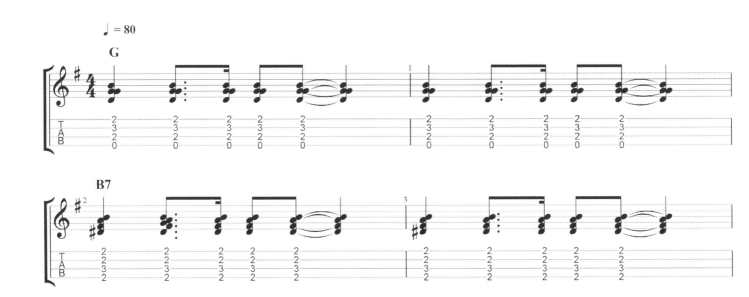

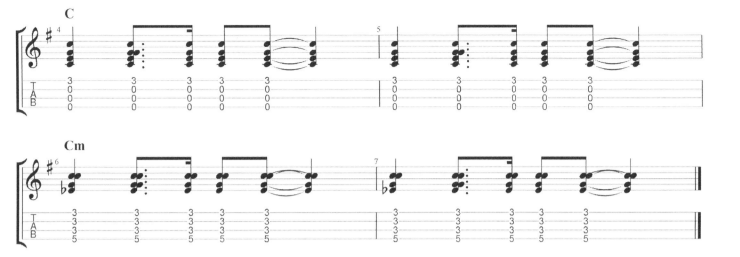

Here is a fun new picking pattern for you to try.

Hold down a D chord.

First pick the fourth string with your thumb (*p*).

Pick the third string with your index finger (*i*).

Pick the first and second strings together with your ring and middle finger (*a* and *m*).

Finally, return to the third string with *i*.

Try this picking pattern on the chord sequence in Example 11e and experiment with it on other sequences you know.

Example 11f

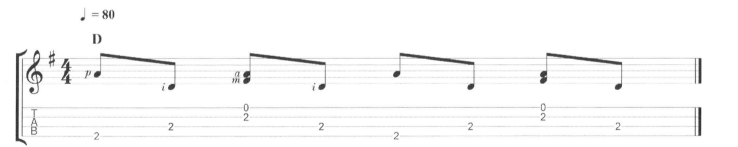

Example 11g combines a picked single note with strummed chords. Alternate the direction of the strums using the symbols to help you.

Example 11g

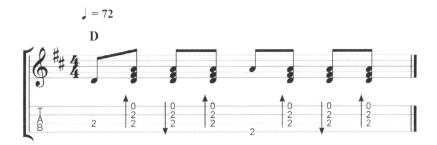

Once you have the picking patterns sounding smooth, clean and confident, try it with this Gm chord.

Gm

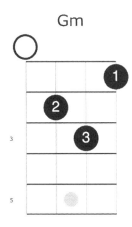

You can use this picking pattern on the song *Aura Lee*. You might recognise it because Elvis recorded it as *Love Me Tender*.

Aura Lee

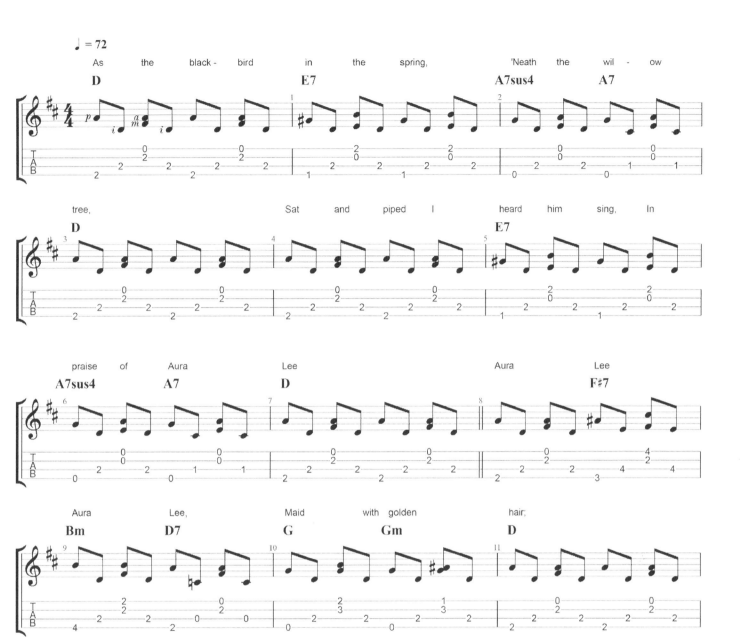

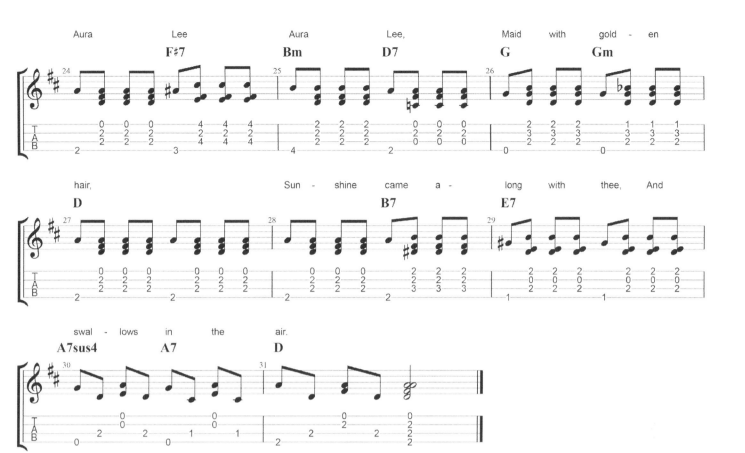

Chapter Twelve: Tricks, Crazy Chords and more!

In this chapter, we'll take a look at some chords and approaches that are less common but can really help to bring a song to life.

Here is a great idea that moves between a D and a Dsus4 chord, that helps bring interest to an otherwise static D Major chord. This is a similar idea to the intro of *Crazy Little Thing Called Love* by Queen.

Hold down the D Major chord, strum it twice, then simply add the fourth finger on the 3rd fret, second string to make the Dsus4. Strum it once and then remove the finger for a final strum.

For the rhythm, count out loud:

"One and, Two and, Three and, Four and" (**Down-up, Down-up**, Miss-**up**, **Down-up**).

Example 12a

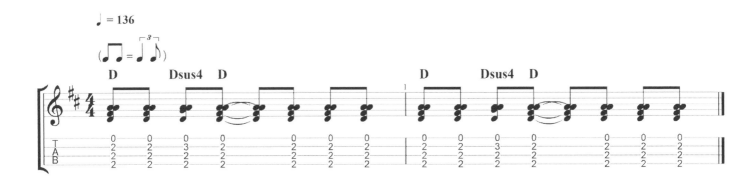

Here is a great idea using both a Dsus4 and a Dsus2 chord. This is used in loads of songs and provides an interesting alternative to what would otherwise be a long period on a D Major chord.

You might have heard this kind of thing in *Brass in Pocket* by the Pretenders or *Merry Christmas* by John Lennon.

Play a D chord, then remove your third finger to create a Dsus2.

Next, add the fourth finger, just as in the previous example, to create Dsus4.

Finally, remove it again and put the third finger back in place to form D Major once again.

Example 12b

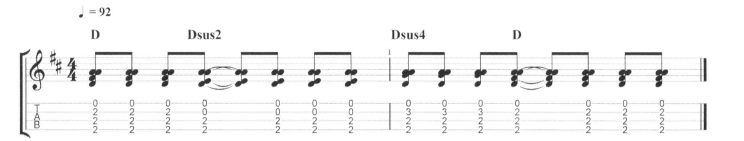

You can easily play the same ideas on a G Major chord, but this time it's your second finger that comes off to create the sus2 chord.

Example 12c

Here is another example of how of moving just one finger can make a static chord vamp more interesting.

Instead of staying on an F Major chord you can change from F to F6.

Then, to turn F6 into FMaj7, place your fourth finger on the 4th fret of the third string.

Example 12d

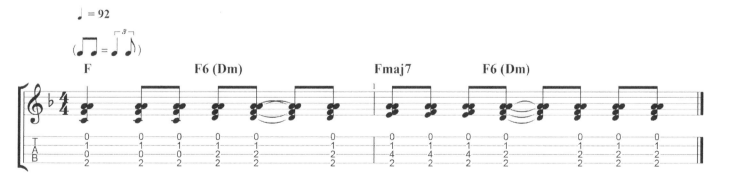

Major 7 (Maj7) chords have a mostly bright, uplifting sound and you'll often find them in more jazzy songs. However, they also pop up in lots of other chord sequences like this one that's similar to *Imagine* by John Lennon.

The movement from C Major to CMaj7 is very easy, just move the note on the first string down one fret.

Example 12e

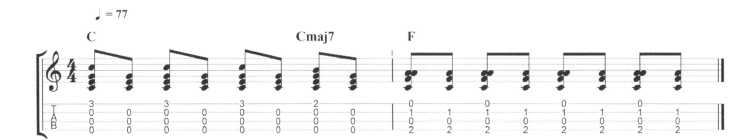

Gmaj7 and Cmaj7 can be combined to create a sequence just like *Waiting in Vain* by Bob Marley. The shape for Gmaj7 is just like the shape for a D chord. Just move everything one string over to the first, second and third string.

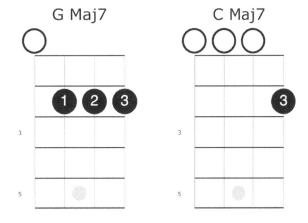

In this example, we only strum on the "and" of the beat, as is common in many reggae songs. Miss the strings on each down stroke and catch them with each up stroke. Count:

"One **and**, Two **and**, Three **and**, Four **and**".

Example 12f

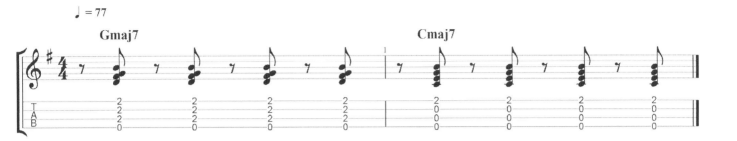

Here are two moveable Maj7 shapes.

Notice that you must *barre* with the third finger for the AMaj7 chord. Flatten it across the strings, while the first finger frets the fourth string.

Example 12g

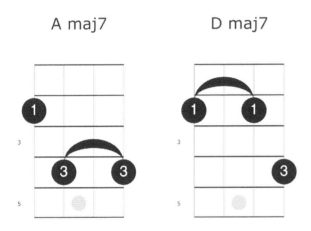

A maj7   D maj7

Next, try this G diminished (G Dim) chord. You'll probably think it sounds a little strange on its own, but in certain chord sequences it can really sound great.

Example 12h

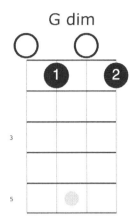

G dim

This diminished chord can be made into a moveable shape very easily:

Example 12i

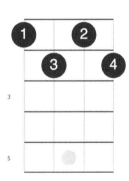

D dim

Diminished chord shapes are sometimes used as substitutes for dominant 7 chords. For example, in *My Sweet Lord* by George Harrison. This trick can add a lot of colour to a chord sequence and create a tense sound on a dominant 7 chord. (Here an F dim is used instead of a C#7)

Example 12j

The Am7 chord is the easiest chord to play on ukulele as it requires no fingers at all!

Example 12k

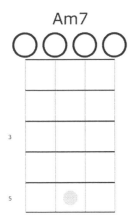

Am7

To make this into a moveable shape, simply bar across all of the strings with the first finger:

Example 12l

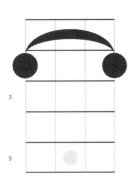

Bm7

Here's one final trick to help add colour to your dominant 7 chords. Instead of changing from C7 straight to F Major, try adding in this Bbm6 chord. You can even replace the C7 with it completely in this instance, and it will function in a similar way to the C7, pulling us back to F.

Obviously, this won't be suitable in every context, but here it adds a nice jazzy feel to an otherwise pretty bland chord change.

Simply barre the first finger across the first, second and third string to play Bbm6.

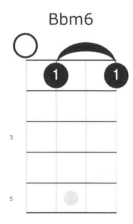

Bbm6

Example 12m

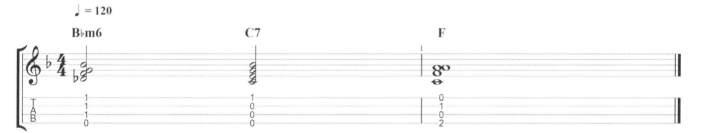

Now learn this mainstay of the uke repertoire, *I'll See You in My Dreams*. It that contains many of the chords and tricks you've learnt in this chapter.

I'll See You in My Dreams

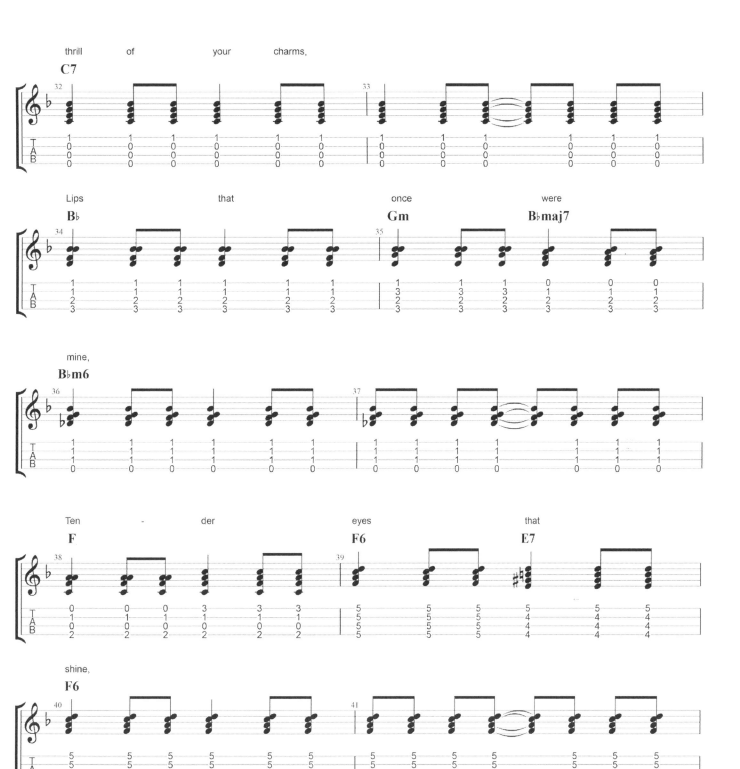

Chapter Thirteen: Finishing Touches

Finally, let's study a few techniques and concepts that I consider to be "finishing touches", which can add a bit of finesse to your playing. They are the little twiddles or *ornaments* that can make an otherwise simple chord pattern into something truly musical.

Start by playing this simple melody on the first string.

Example 13a

Now play the same melody, but instead of picking the open string, sound it by *pulling off* the string with the fretting hand from the 2nd fret that you just picked. This movement is called a *pull-off*.

Example 13b

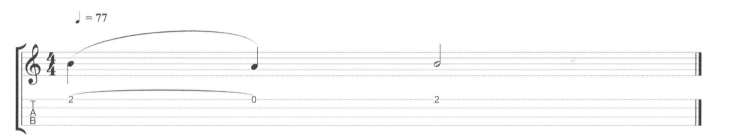

Next, *hammer* the second finger back on to the 2nd fret to make it sound again *without* picking the string. This movement is called a *hammer-on*. Try all of the movements in one smooth motion. Listen to the audio to hear what you're aiming for.

Pick the first note on the second fret, pull off to sound the open string, then hammer on with the same finger to sound the 3rd fret again. You'll play three notes, but only pick once. See how smooth and even you can make the three notes sound.

Example 13c

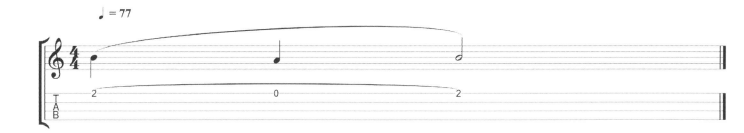

Once you have this pattern sounding clear, try it while holding a G Major chord.

Strum the chord then allow the notes to ring as you perform the pull-off, then the hammer on the first string.

Example 13d

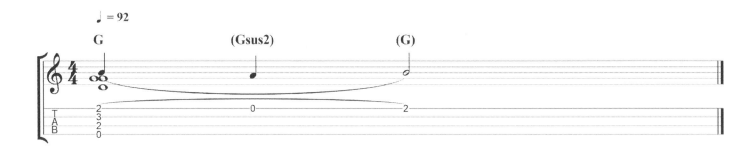

Now try this finger picking pattern that contains a pull-off on the first string.

Pick through the G Major chord using *p*, *i*, *m* then *a* on each of the four strings, as you've done before.

On the first string, pull off from the 2nd fret to the open string.

Pick with *m* on the second string then finish with *i* on the third string.

Example 13e

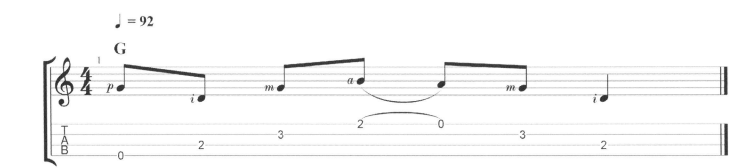

These *ornaments* are an extremely effective way of adding a melodic element to a chord sequence and you can normally find ways to add them to any chord.

Consider a chord pattern like G, C, D.

Example 13f

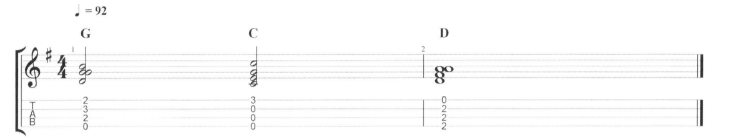

Using the ideas from Example 13e, it could easily be turned into something like this.

Example 13g

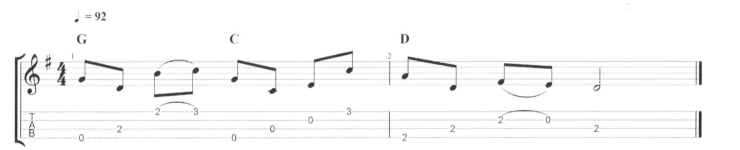

Or, once you're very confident, even something like this next example, which includes a rapid hammer-on and pull-off on beat two. Listen to the audio to get the feel of the pattern before you play it.

Example 13h

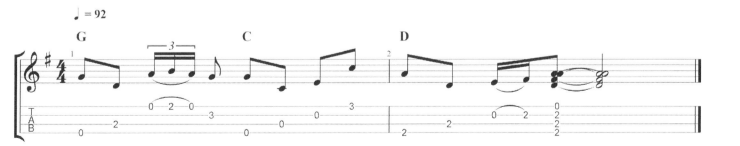

And finally, try this technical study that combines most of the approaches we have looked at in this book. There's a lot here, so you'll need to break it down bar by bar. Pay attention to playing clean chords, good rhythmic strumming, and playing the hammer-ons and pull-offs in time.

As always, listen to the audio and learn this piece slowly with a metronome before speeding up.

Good luck!

Technical Study

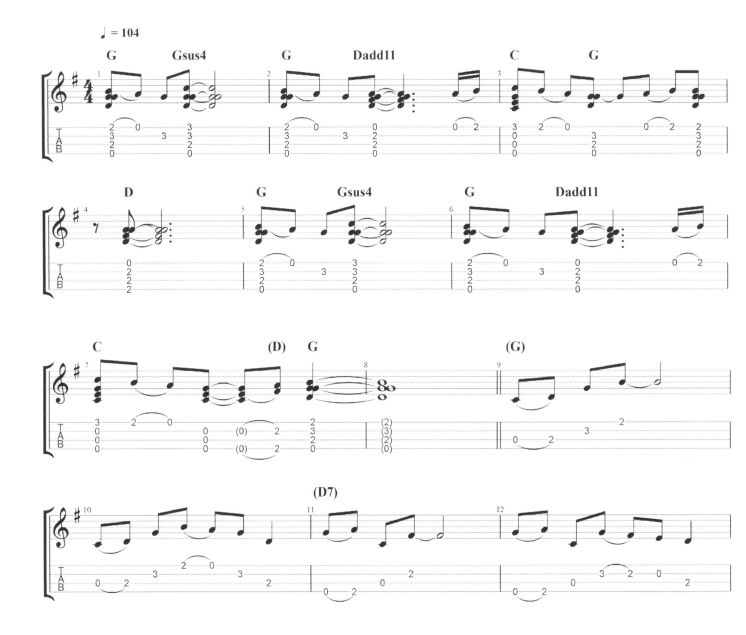

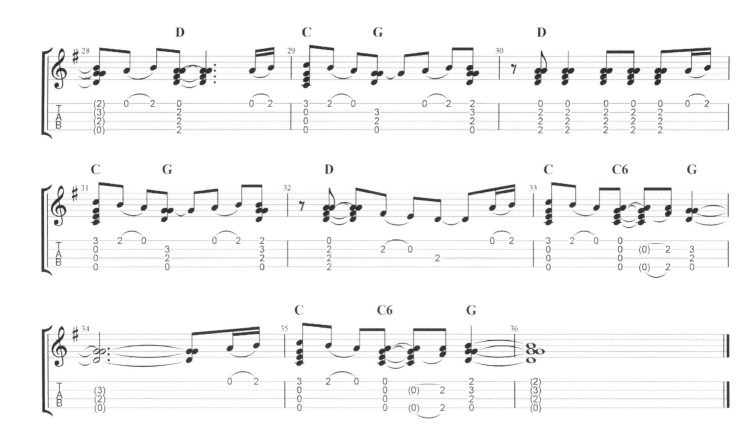

Chord Dictionary and Closing Words

The following pages contain diagrams of pretty much every chord you'll ever need to know on the ukulele.

There are just 12 notes in music and I've included nine of the most important chords you'll come across for each one. This creates a palette of 108 (9 x 12) chords to choose from! However, some are *much* more common than others.

You should definitely know the Major, Minor, 7, Maj7 and Min7 voicings for the most common keys of C, G, A, D and E.

To save you time, I suggest that you don't bother to learn the Diminished and Augmented chords at all, just refer back to this dictionary if you ever come across one in a song.

Above all, the best way to learn chords (just like learning a new word) is to use it in context. That boils down to simply learning lots of songs on the ukulele and you'll quickly see that the same common chords crop up over and over again.

The ukulele is an uncomplicated instrument and is best suited to a fairly limited range of keys. Most of these keys have quite a few chords in common, so it's not surprising that the same ones crop up all the time – they're just particularly suited for the uke!

This all goes to show that with a bit of work, focused in the right areas, learning the ukulele can be quite easy and once you know the common chords, you'll be able to play anything you want to fairly quickly.

If you can't find the chords for a song you want to play on ukulele, try looking for a guitar or easy piano version of the song, as these often have the chords written over the top of the music.

My best advice is to use your ears as much as possible. You'll hear similar strumming patterns and chord sequences used over and over again. With a little effort, learning ukulele will quickly become a skill that you can enjoy for years into the future.

Have fun!

Daryl

C Chords

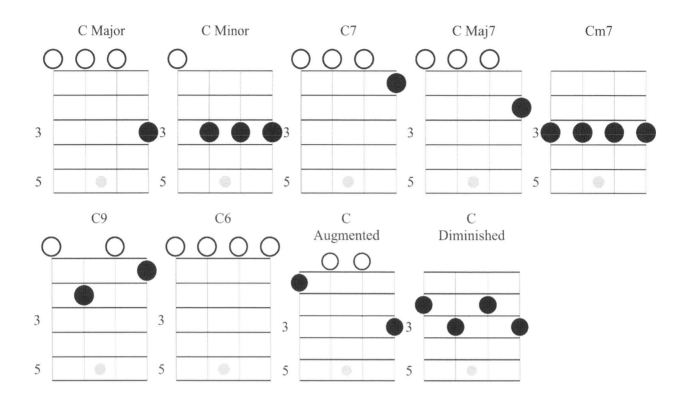

Db / C# Chords

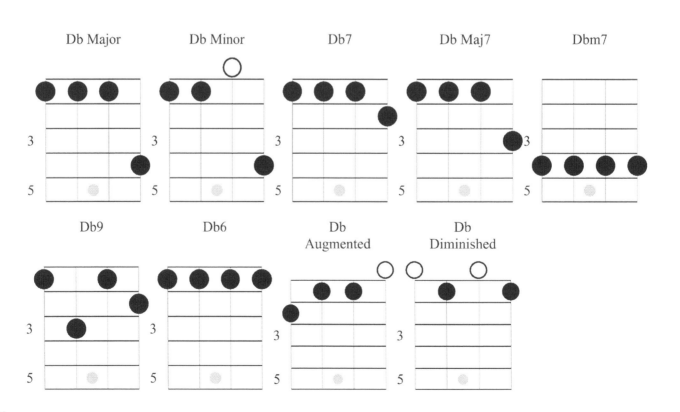

D Chords

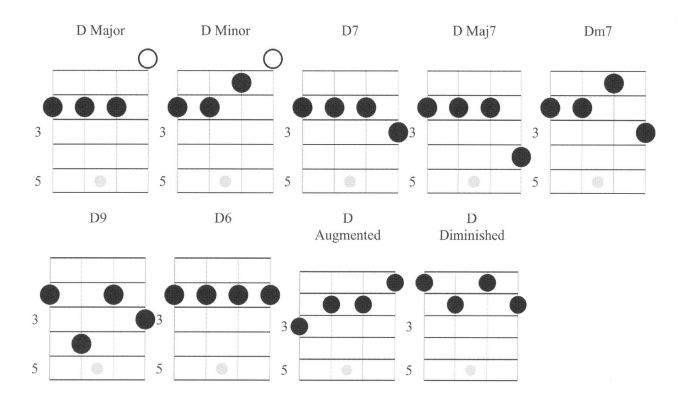

D# / Eb Chords

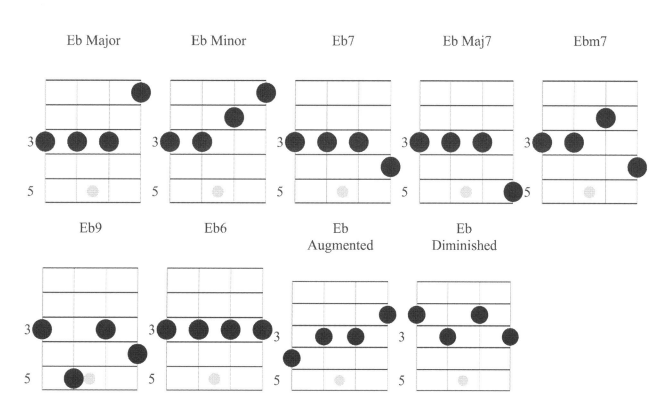

E Chords

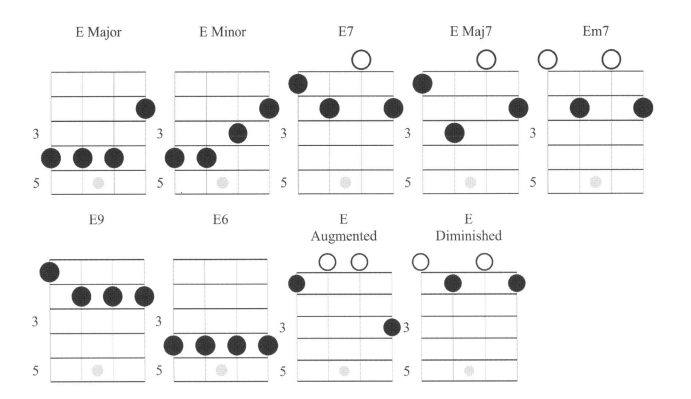

F Chords

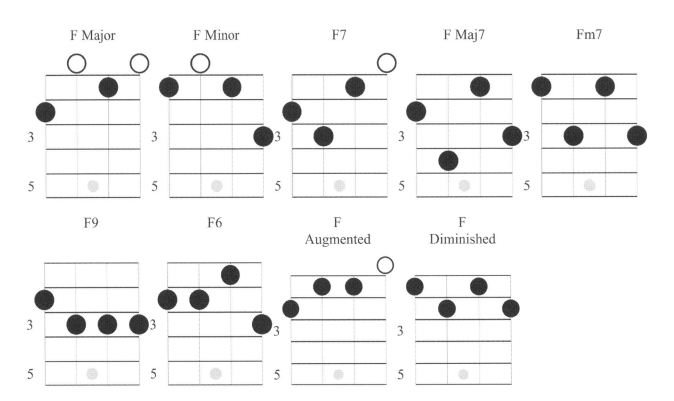

F# / Gb Chords

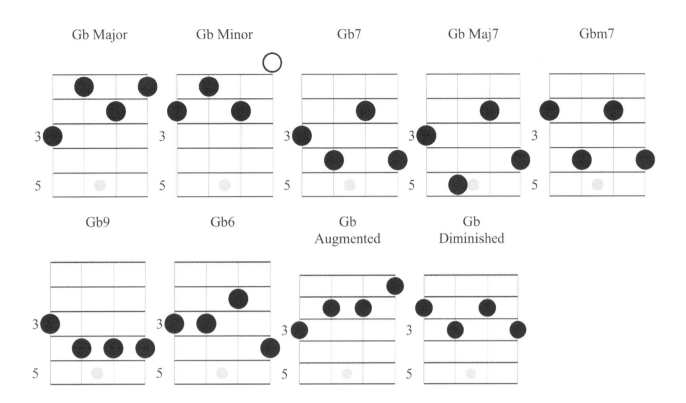

G Chords

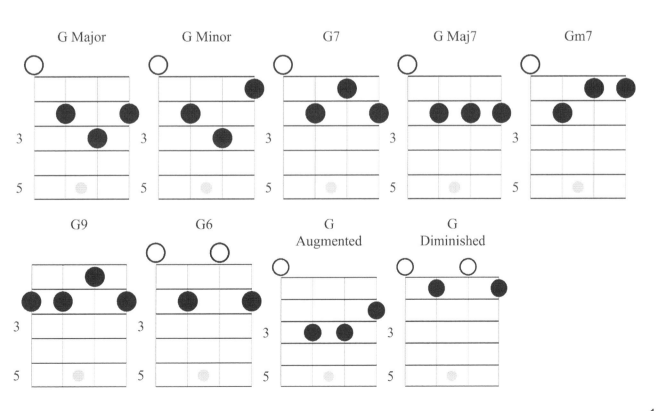

G# / Ab Chords

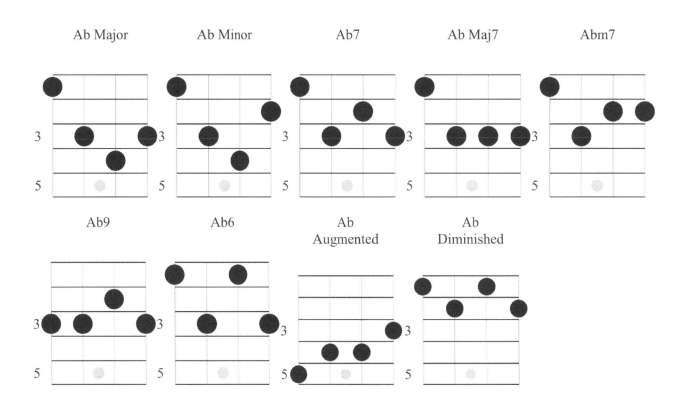

Ab Major Ab Minor Ab7 Ab Maj7 Abm7

Ab9 Ab6 Ab Augmented Ab Diminished

A Chords

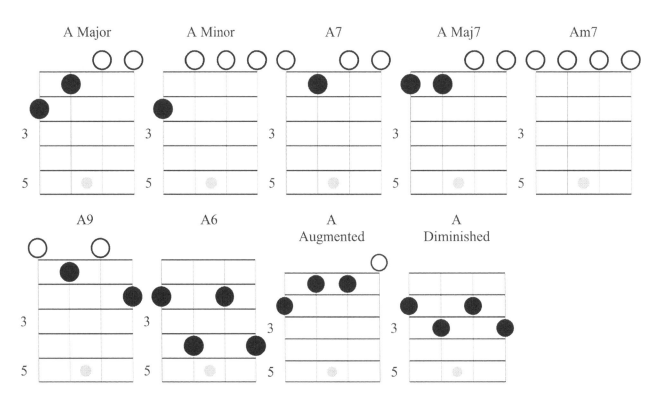

A Major A Minor A7 A Maj7 Am7

A9 A6 A Augmented A Diminished

A# / Bb Chords

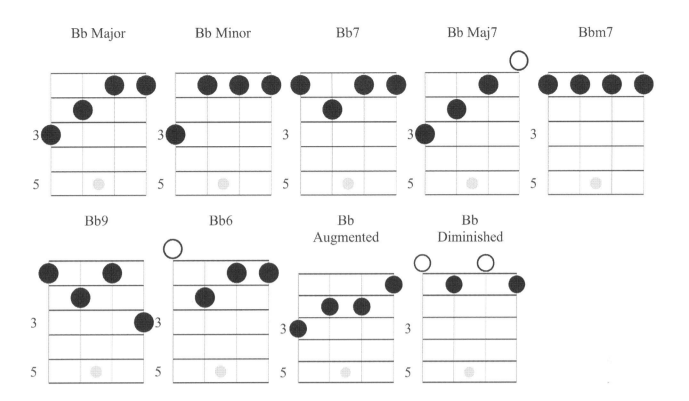

B Chords

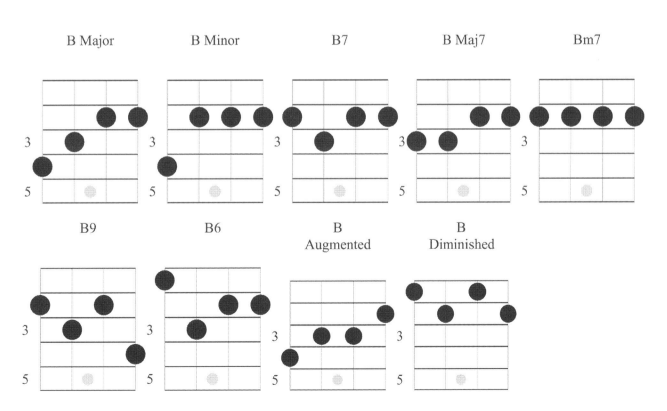